CELEBRATING
SMALL
VICTORIES

CELEBRATING SMALL VICTORIES

A Counselor's Manual for Treating Chronic Mental Illness and Substance Abuse

Ken Montrose, M.A.
Dennis Daley, Ph.D.

 HAZELDEN®

Hazelden
Center City, Minnesota 55012-0176

©1995 by Hazelden Foundation
All rights reserved. Published 1995
(Formerly titled *Celebrating Small Victories: A Primer of Approaches
and Attitudes for Helping Clients with Dual Disorders*)
Printed in the United States of America
No portion of this publication may be reproduced in any manner
without the written permission of the publisher

Library of Congress Cataloging-in-Publication Data
Montrose, Ken.
 Celebrating small victories: a counselor's manual for treating
chronic mental illness and substance abuse / Ken Montrose, Dennis Daley.
  p. cm.
 Includes bibliographical references and index.
 ISBN 1-56838-092-5
 1. Dual diagnosis. I. Daley, Dennis C. II. Title.
RC564.68.M66 1995
616.89'1—dc20   95-18958
                                                                    CIP

Editor's note
Hazelden offers a variety of information on chemical dependency and related areas. Our publications do not necessarily represent Hazelden's programs, nor do they officially speak for any Twelve Step organization.

The personal stories in this book are composites of many individuals. Any resemblance to any one person, living or dead, is strictly coincidental.

The Twelve Steps of AA and Twelve Traditions of AA are reprinted and adapted with permission of Alcoholics Anonymous World Services, Inc. The excerpt from *The A.A. Member—Medications and Other Drugs* is reprinted with permission of Alcoholics Anonymous World Services, Inc. Permission to reprint and adapt this material does not mean that AA has reviewed or approved the contents of this publication, nor that AA agrees with the views expressed herein. AA is a program of recovery from alcoholism—use of the Twelve Steps and Twelve Traditions in connection with programs and activities which are patterned after AA, but which address other problems, does not imply otherwise.

CONTENTS

PREFACE

We have written this book especially for people new to treating mental illness and substance abuse. If you are a casemanager, program aide, residential counselor, paraprofessional, or volunteer, this book will provide you with practical treatment guidelines and strategies for working with consumers. If you are a nurse, doctor, administrator, or clinician who has some experience working in the mental health and substance abuse fields, this book will offer you fresh insight into treating both mental illness and substance abuse simultaneously.

The people we describe are not the "worried well." They are people who suffer from what the "Big Book" of Alcoholics Anonymous calls "grave emotional and mental disorders" (Alcoholics Anonymous World Services 1976). These people may have difficulty in many facets of their lives. Frequently they may be hospitalized; they often resist the treatment they desperately need. They may have been in state mental institutions or jails. Their *current* ability to function in the community may be quite limited due to their mental illnesses and substance abuse. Their *potential* ability is yet unknown. We describe the people who are "worst off," knowing that they may be capable of functioning far better than they function now. With help, they often make astounding recoveries.

We have not focused on any one diagnosis. The interventions described can be used by most professionals in most settings. We have kept the interventions simple and concrete so they can be used for a variety of problems.

Many pages of this book are devoted to the effect of staff attitudes on treatment. This may seem at odds with the book's claim to be a "how-to" book. However, we believe the most important component of treatment is a consistent, nonjudgmental, and positive attitude. All other treatment components depend on maintaining such an attitude.

You have little control over who finds stability and serenity; but you can control, and therefore change, your attitude. If you want to help people overcome mental illness and substance abuse, you need to accept your limitations, not personalize resistance, and judge your efforts appropriately. These things are much easier to do than "getting" someone to abstain from substances. Assessing and changing your own attitude is the perfect starting point.

Language has particular importance when talking about people with mental illness and substance abuse. Advocates for the mentally ill have lobbied to call people receiving mental health services *consumers;* we use this term and the term *client* to refer to people involved in outpatient services. We only use the term *patient* to mean someone being treated as an inpatient in a psychiatric hospital.

It is ironic that we cannot use the word *drug* to mean all drugs, since alcohol can be as harmful as any other drug. Unfortunately, when many of us see the word *drug,* an extra neuron has to fire to include alcohol. Hence, we use the word *drug* to mean any drug other than alcohol. We refer to alcohol specifically and to certain drugs specifically. We use the word *substance* to mean alcohol and other drugs.

Throughout the book we use the terms *abstinence* and *compliance.* *Abstinence* means no use of substances, including cold and flu preparations, that contain alcohol. It also means no use of substances on special occasions and no use of self-prescribed chemicals for "medicinal purposes." It means using prescribed medications exactly as prescribed. It means taking over-the-counter medications only as directed. (Taking twice the recommended dose of Benadryl to fall asleep is a form of substance abuse.) Most important, it means the consumer never getting a prescription from a doctor or dentist who is not fully aware of his addiction.

We use the term *compliance* to mean compliance with medications. It is important for the consumer to take psychotropic medications as prescribed. We do not, however, suggest he have blind faith. The consumer should have the opportunity—he certainly has the right—to negotiate medication levels. Only the consumer really knows how the medications make him feel. No matter how beneficial or how harmful, he has to live with their effect. By *compliance* we mean a negotiated compliance.

We avoid the term *addict* to describe someone who uses/abuses substances. People who have been chronically mentally ill have a disease that prevents them from using substances safely. We believe any substance use constitutes abuse for someone coping with a serious mental illness. Substance use almost always makes a mental illness worse. Thankfully, many people discover that once they quit using substances, they can manage their mental illnesses. Whether a consumer is addicted is not the issue. Doing everything possible to overcome a mental illness is much more important than deciding whether someone's *use* is *abuse* or *addiction*.

To avoid sexist language and repeatedly using *the consumer,* we alternate the use of *he* and *she* to describe consumers.

INTRODUCTION

Imagine sitting in a rowboat in shark-infested water just offshore from two islands. On the larger one, TGIF Island, people laugh and indulge in all manners of hedonistic pleasures. TGIF lies just above sea level, and now and then a wave carries some of the revelers off the island to the hungry sharks. No one seems to notice.

Next to TGIF is a smaller island, Recovery Island. It has a narrow beach jutting out from sheer cliff walls. Carved into the walls are a series of steps that lead to several plateaus. People on Recovery Island enjoy all manners of sober pursuits. They call from the plateaus to the people on their beach. Some heed the call and start climbing the steps to the first plateau. Others stay on the beach and, from time to time, some are swept back into the water.

Many of the people in the water swim furiously for one of the islands. Some make it; others are devoured by sharks. Still others swim off in the wrong direction or swim in circles. Some are oblivious to the danger and float in the water with their eyes shut and their minds occupied with things beyond a horizon only they see.

Your job is to get as many of these people as possible out of the water. Sadly, many want to be left alone and are even hostile when approached. Most of the people want to be taken to TGIF Island. Several complain bitterly when asked to help row, expecting to be rescued, not put to work. You realize all this paddling around is exhausting. Helping these people seems pointless—let the sharks have their fill.

It is then that you recognize several people you have helped making the arduous climb up the steps of Recovery Island. Some are helped by people who are not put off by their different thoughts or strange dress. You paddle on, trying to help more people get out of the water.

The trick is to keep paddling no matter how tough your job seems. Overcoming mental illness and substance abuse is difficult.

Diagnoses are often unclear, and problems tend to pile up for both the consumer and the treatment professional. For example, what can be done for someone coping with mental illness and substance abuse who just got out of prison, who has just discovered he is HIV positive, and who wants to be *paid* to participate in treatment? It is hard enough just dealing with schizophrenia, bipolar disorder, major depression, and other major mental illnesses. Throw in substance abuse, and recovery from both illnesses may seem like an impossible dream. It becomes easy to forget how many heroic people are indeed climbing the steps on Recovery Island.

Celebrating Small Victories outlines a few simple guidelines for treating mental illness and substance abuse. Several chapters discuss interventions. The importance of repeating basic information with the consumer, of being enthusiastic, and of celebrating small victories cannot be overemphasized.

Your job is simple: keep paddling.

PART I

MENTAL ILLNESS AND SUBSTANCE ABUSE:
A DIFFERENT VIEW

v

CHAPTER 1

TREATMENT DILEMMAS

It has only been within the last five to ten years that treatment systems have seen the wisdom of integrating services for people coping with mental illness and substance abuse. In the past, a consumer's difficulties were viewed as the "real" problem and the "other" problem. The real problem was whatever the clinic where we worked happened to treat. The other problem was whatever the clinic had no idea how to treat.

If a program specialized in substance abuse treatment, then the symptoms of mental illness were the other problem. Substance abuse was treated as the real problem. Many symptoms associated with a mental illness were written off as something that would pass, or evidence that the consumer was not "working" the Twelve Steps properly. "She's not really depressed; she's wallowing in self-pity," treatment professionals would be inclined to say. "She needs to go to more AA meetings and focus on other alcoholics."

On the other hand, mental health professionals tended to view substance abuse as just a symptom of mental illness and not the real problem. "Treat the real problem," they said, "and the need to use substances will disappear." Or "She's not really addicted. Spending her whole check on cocaine is just her way of coping with her feelings of inadequacy and depression."

As professionals, sometimes we could no longer ignore the "other" problem. As it became clear that a consumer was not improving, a referral to that "other" agency where they know how to deal with the other problem would be considered. Sometimes the consumer had the other problem so badly that treatment professionals lamented that she was causing intense discomfort most noticeable in the seat of the pants. We were all too happy to refer her to other professionals.

Sadly, many people got lost between agencies. A consumer might get conflicting messages from mental health and substance abuse treatment professionals. She might be told that once her psychotropic medications were adjusted, she would not feel compelled to use alcohol and other drugs. She might also be told that she was not really in recovery while she was taking any drugs, no matter who prescribed them.

Finally it occurred to both systems to treat the whole person, in the same place, with the same people, at the same time. This has not always been easy.

The treatment professional faces three problems that are more severe for people coping with both problems than for those who are coping with one. The first problem is that the diagnosis is often unclear. The second is that mental illness and substance abuse in combination often cause more physical, psychological, and spiritual damage than either causes alone. The third problem is that recovery from both can be more difficult than recovery from either one alone.

What is the diagnosis?

One of the most difficult aspects of treating mental illness and substance abuse is arriving at a diagnosis. Often the consumer's symptoms change from day to day. It may not be clear whether he has a mental illness, is abusing substances, is withdrawing from substances, has some unknown physiological disorder, or all of the above. A good strategy to deal with this is to formulate a *working diagnosis.*

A working diagnosis is what you believe to be the correct diagnosis based on the most accurate information currently available. This diagnosis changes as the consumer's condition or the information known about his condition changes.

Hidden factors may make your working diagnosis inaccurate. A consumer can hide his use of substances or can even hide his psychiatric symptoms. Expect to get fooled, lied to, or honestly misled by someone who does not believe he has a problem, or is too delusional or otherwise impaired to know what the problem is.

CASE ILLUSTRATION 1: DIAGNOSTIC DIFFICULTIES

Greg complained of being extremely anxious. He had difficulty falling asleep and reported feeling "nervous" and "jumpy" during the day. It was difficult for him to sit through a group therapy session. Most days he could be seen pacing the halls of the clinic. He had a fine tremor in his hands that he could not consciously control.

Greg told everyone involved in his treatment that he was taking his Haldol at lunch and before bedtime, exactly as prescribed. He had been on a slightly lower dose of Haldol while he was an inpatient, but he requested an increase two weeks after his discharge. He denied taking any illegal stimulants and none were found through a urine drug screen. His anxiety usually got worse after lunch, as he was sitting on the bus on his way to the drop-in center.

Greg reported that he felt "fine" when he got up in the morning. He reported feeling little or no anxiety until he got on the bus at 1 P.M. each day. From that time until he fell asleep, he experienced restlessness and anxiety. According to Greg, it did not matter where he was or what he was doing, he felt "jumpy" from one o'clock on. Greg denied having any fear of specific situations, people, or places.

At first it was suspected that he had akathisia, which is sometimes a side effect of neuroleptic medication. Akathisia is marked by restlessness and involuntary bodily movement. People suffering from akathisia often complain of being unable to sit still. Akathisia can greatly increase a consumer's anxiety.

Greg repeatedly asked for something to "calm his nerves." He balked when it was suggested his Haldol be reduced. "You're really dying to get me back in the hospital, aren't you?" he asked. He was, however, willing to try Cogentin, a drug that can greatly decrease the side effects that sometimes result from taking neuroleptics.

After three weeks of taking Cogentin, Greg was as restless as before. He finally agreed to a reduction in medications while he continued to take the Cogentin. A month after his medications were reduced, he still felt no better. The working diagnosis, "akathisia," had to be reconsidered. (The working diagnosis does not have to be a formal DSM-IV diagnosis—it is more of a description of what you think is wrong. It can include family stress, work pressures, physical ailments, and the like.)

Without discarding the old working diagnosis, a new one was considered. Several people involved in his treatment argued that Greg was suffering from an anxiety disorder. Greg's psychiatrist wanted him to begin a cognitive-behavioral program designed to reduce his anxiety. In conjunction with this, Greg would be prescribed an antianxiety drug.

Greg refused to consider the program: "I've been through those programs. They tell you to tighten all your muscles and picture yourself lying on a beach." But he readily agreed to take the drug: "Make sure you give me the brand-name stuff. I don't like the generic. Don't start me on the 'halfs' cause they don't do anything and I end up taking a whole milligram of it anyway. Could you make it Klonopin? That seems to work the best."

A week after he started taking Ativan, an antianxiety agent, he ran into a staff member at a local convenience store. Greg was refilling a thirty-two-ounce coffee mug. The two cups of coffee Greg had reported drinking each day totaled sixty-four ounces of coffee. In talking with other staff at the community residential rehabilitation center and the drop-in center, the staff member discovered that Greg frequently took walks in the direction of convenience stores. It finally dawned on everyone that he might be going there to refill his thirty-two-ounce coffee mug.

Greg eventually admitted to drinking eight to ten thirty-two-ounce mugs of coffee each day. The working diagnosis was changed to "caffeinism," and Greg was taken off Ativan. He continued to gulp alarming amounts of coffee despite every effort to help him reduce his consumption to two cups per day. Rather than picture himself at the beach, he asked if he could visualize himself standing tall on a mountainside—surrounded by coffee beans and coca plants.

The Point Is . . .

1. You may never have all the information you need.
2. Even a legal drug, such as caffeine, can be abused.
3. Drug abuse, in this case caffeine, exacerbates and mimics symptoms of mental illness.

Mental illness: a predisposition to use?

Mental illnesses by themselves can be devastating to the consumer, her family and friends. Imagine what it would be like to have a particular mental illness and how substance abuse might affect that illness. To do this, answer five questions about the various mental illnesses:

1. How much worse would someone with this disorder be under the influence of alcohol or other drugs?
2. How tempting would alcohol or other drugs be to someone with this disorder?
3. How likely is it that this individual would be able to control her use of alcohol or other drugs?

4. Could I or the consumer confuse the use of alcohol and other drugs with a mental disorder?

5. Could I or the consumer confuse the withdrawal from alcohol or other drugs with a mental disorder?

Brief descriptions of common mental illnesses are offered here. (For a thorough review of the clinical criteria necessary to make a diagnosis, see the recommended reading.)

Thought disorders such as schizophrenia strike one in a hundred adults. Schizophrenia is marked by delusions in which the person arrives at strange conclusions based upon faulty logic. For example, a woman may believe that the stories on the evening news have some special message intended only for her (idea of reference). She may have grandiose delusions, such as believing that she gets these messages because she is "the chosen one." Her delusions may be persecutory. She may believe that the anchorwoman on the news is secretly threatening her.

A consumer with schizophrenia may experience hallucinations, most often auditory and referred to as *voices.* She will often hear these voices outside her head. They are distinctly different from her own thoughts. Sometimes the voices are friendly but many times they are not.

People with schizophrenia often have difficulty making sense of the world. Their emotions may not be tied to their experiences. They may feel a complete absence of emotions, energy, or connectedness with the world around them. When acutely ill they may act bizarrely.

Mood disorders can include feeling overly energetic, as in *mania,* or drained as in *depression.* Mania is characterized by rapid speech, little need for sleep, racing thoughts, high energy, and poor judgment. People suffering from mania are apt to go on spending sprees, make poor decisions, start impossible projects or start many projects, or put themselves in danger.

Depression is the opposite of mania. A depressed consumer often feels a loss of energy. She may feel sad, hopeless, and helpless.

She may become so despondent that she plans or attempts suicide.

Some people swing between the two extremes and suffer from *bipolar disorder*. These changes in functioning can happen without warning and without an easily identifiable cause.

Anxiety disorders are characterized by worry, dread, and a number of physical symptoms. The consumer suffering from *generalized anxiety disorder* may experience these symptoms to some degree most of her waking hours. She may complain of an inescapable feeling of impending doom.

Phobias are another common anxiety disorder in which a consumer develops an irrational fear of a particular place or situation. As she approaches, or in some cases even thinks about, the feared situation or place, she may become overwhelmed with anxiety and panic. The consumer may experience rapid heartbeat, shortness of breath, sweating, dizziness, and blurred vision. She may then avoid that situation, often to her detriment. The more situations she avoids, the more withdrawn she becomes.

Agoraphobia limits where the consumer will travel. The consumer may fear any situation where she feels trapped. This can include riding in a car, taking public transportation, crossing a bridge, driving through a tunnel, or riding in an elevator. Some people with agoraphobia become housebound.

Panic disorder can be a part of agoraphobia. The panic-stricken consumer will suffer "attacks" of intense terror. It is common for the panic-prone person to fear dying, losing control, or going crazy. A racing heart, sweating, feelings of unreality, dizziness, and nausea are all common symptoms of panic attacks.

Someone who repeats the same ritualistic behavior over and over may be suffering from *obsessive-compulsive disorder*. The consumer with obsessive-compulsive disorder may perform elaborate rituals, such as checking all the locks in her house in a certain order ten times before leaving. She does this to avoid the anxiety she feels when she does not do so.

A *personality disorder* involves a group of behaviors related to personality traits that cause the consumer great personal distress or interfere with her ability to get along with others. These traits are usually rigid, ingrained, and long lasting. In Twelve Step programs, such traits are referred to as *character defects*. Although there are too many personality disorders to discuss here, most consumers afflicted with the disorders experience the following:

- They have difficulty developing and maintaining relationships with others.
- They have trouble seeing their personality problems and often attribute their problems to other people, bad luck, or unfortunate circumstances.
- They have trouble dealing with their feelings, especially painful ones.
- They show traits that are either over- or underdeveloped.

For example, the consumer with antisocial personality disorder may act only to satisfy her own needs, showing little concern for others. People with obsessive-compulsive traits are often fixated on rules and order, and are not very playful or spontaneous. The most common personality disorders seen with addiction include borderline, antisocial, and "mixed," which involves clusters of traits from several different personality disorders.

CASE ILLUSTRATION 2: EPISODES OF MENTAL ILLNESS
AND SUBSTANCE ABUSE

Manny suffers from bipolar disorder. He enjoys his manic episodes and the feeling of being up. When he is in the manic stage of his illness, he abuses substances. He believes he is invincible at these times and he throws caution to the wind. He hates taking lithium, a mood stabilizer commonly used to treat bipolar disorder.

He complains of a "slow, heavy" feeling on lithium. When he takes it as prescribed, his life is manageable and by his own report enjoyable, if not exciting.

Manny's troubles usually begin after he has been stable for months or longer. He begins to feel more and more in control of his life. It occurs to him that "now that things have settled down," he may not need the lithium anymore. Sometimes he tapers off the lithium; other times he just stops taking it. By the time he is out of control again, his thinking is too rapid and grandiose for him to comprehend he is in danger.

During his last manic episode, Manny made a number of poor choices. He had a sexual liaison with a prostitute. Manny acquired a sexually transmitted disease, which he later passed on to his wife. He tried cocaine and was arrested for fighting in a bar. He took money from his own business and bought strange chemicals by the barrel because he believed he had the formula for "flexible concrete," a product he thought of while his mind was in a "hyperborealic continuum."

Two weeks after this episode he was served with divorce papers while on a pass from a psychiatric hospital. His business partner started legal proceedings of his own against Manny. Traces of opiates were found in his blood, but Manny has no recollection of how they got there.

He was barely over withdrawal from the chemicals he had ingested when reality set in. Manny made his first suicide attempt the day he was released from the hospital.

The Point Is . . .

1. Many people do not abuse substances except when they are experiencing symptoms of their mental illness.

2. Reality can be depressing. Fortunately, professionals can help people break the cycle of symptoms and substance abuse by teaching them to cope with reality.

——◆◆◆——

Alcohol and other drugs

Keeping in mind the pain mental illness can cause, you should try to imagine how appealing the following groups of chemicals might be to someone with a mental illness.

Depressants like alcohol, barbiturates, opiates, and analgesics reduce anxiety. They can induce sleep and a feeling of well-being.

Hallucinogens like LSD and psilocybin can alter the perception of reality. The boundaries of time and self can seem to fade away. They provide an external explanation for an unpredictable inner world.

Stimulants like cocaine and amphetamines cause feelings of boundless energy, euphoria, confidence. They can reduce the need for sleep and can reduce appetite.

The allure of alcohol and other drugs can be very strong. Whether or not a mental illness is present, how many people do not want to enjoy a sense of well-being and boundless energy? How many of us would like to escape from the pressures and disappointments of everyday life for a while? In the short term, people like the way substances make them feel. If cocaine made people anxious and paranoid the first several times they tried it, they would not keep buying it. On the other hand, if cocaine lifted their mood, gave them more energy, and made sex more intense, they might want to use it over and over. The allure of drugs is that initially they provide some positive feeling. Although most people realize that there is a price to be paid for this positive feeling, many substances still have a strong appeal.

Some of the substances' allure is cultural. In our society we convince each other that using alcohol and other drugs is glamorous, exciting, relaxing, and part of "growing up." Some mental health workers even argue against stressing abstinence to young consumers.

They believe some consumers are already set apart from their peers and asking them not to use substances will only tend to further isolate them. This is a mistake. Treatment should show young consumers that not using substances is healthy and in their best interest.

Another part of the appeal of substances is the consumer's desire to self-medicate. It is common for a consumer to use a substance to treat unpleasant symptoms of mental illness. In the short term a substance may make the consumer's anxiety, depression, insomnia, or other symptoms more tolerable. To the consumer, even a brief escape from these problems may seem like a bargain, regardless of what his use of a substance will cost.

Sometimes a consumer will take a drug that makes his symptoms worse. The consumer coping with schizophrenia who uses stimulants or hallucinogens is a good example. His chief complaint is that he hears voices. Stimulants make the voices worse, yet he uses them every chance he gets. Why? Partly because using stimulants gives him a false sense of control. He can say to himself, "The voices are just a side effect of the drugs I took" rather than having to say, "I may have a serious mental illness." He may feel more in control of his use of substances than of a mental illness.

Recovery

Recovering from years of substance abuse can be difficult for anyone, but it is especially hard for someone suffering from a mental illness. In addition to dealing with the problems caused by substance abuse, the consumer must deal with the problems caused by mental illness.

The consumer suffering from a mood or anxiety disorder may have no idea what Narcotics Anonymous or Alcoholics Anonymous members mean by *serenity*. One consumer remarked that while she had no idea what serenity felt like, she had a good idea what anxiety was like and she had no intention of facing it sober.

The consumer with a thought disorder may have difficulty understanding that she has either a mental illness or a problem with substance abuse. As a treatment provider, you may wonder if her paranoia is caused by schizophrenia or cocaine abuse. She wonders why you keep looking at her that way, why you keep asking her about her cocaine use. Is it paranoia if the counselors really are trying to "nail you"?

As someone coping with mental illness and addiction begins to recover from both illnesses, her life comes into sharper focus. She has a clearer understanding of what has happened to her and begins to appreciate how much work needs to be done if she is to reclaim her life. Sadly, she may see that she has two highly stigmatized illnesses to deal with.

It may be difficult to help someone who feels so overwhelmed. But before you give up helping people recover, think about this: The harder it is to acquire something, the harder people tend to fight to hold on to it. Experience shows that people who get clean go to great lengths to stay clean. Even consumers hospitalized in an acute psychotic episode—who had a previous history of substance abuse—do not always use substances even during the episode. As reality slips further and further away, they hold on to the understanding that substance use will only make it worse, and come what may, they are not going to pick up a drug.

Don't paddle away. Despite all the problems connected with treating mental illness and substance abuse, consumers do get better. And the transformation they make can be inspiring.

CHAPTER 2

SELLING RECOVERY

Treatment professionals compete for the attention and lives of consumers. When someone leaves our offices they reenter a world floating in chemicals. Drug dealers employ salespeople who make used car salesmen look passive. Pushing abstinence from drugs and participation in treatment can be an uphill battle. Several notions should be addressed aggressively in treatment.

Selling street drugs vs. "selling" recovery

The dealer may be selling a drug like crack, the effects of which have been compared to a fifteen-minute, whole-body orgasm. On the other hand, drugs used to treat mental illness can cause dry mouth, constipation, blurred vision, and other unpleasant side effects. Few consumers will knock over tables, lie, cheat, scam, or spend what little money they have to get psychotropic medications.

A first step in selling recovery is to teach consumers about the long-term negative effects of street drugs and the positive effects of psychotropic medications. Smoking crack may initially provide that feeling of whole-body orgasm, but it may also create medical, psychological, and social problems that are painful and enduring. Many people would not be "chronically" mentally ill if they did not use alcohol and other drugs. Teach consumers that abstaining from substances and complying with mental health treatment can lead to a more stable, rewarding life.

In the general public, people cling to the notion that alcohol is somehow different from other drugs. Some ignore the effects of their use and focus instead on the status of their drug of choice. Alcohol is legal and accepted by most of society. Most other drugs are illegal and not as accepted. People use this logic to justify their alcohol abuse: "Sure I'm covered in my own vomit, but at least I'm not in jail like some drug addict!"

Although it is a gross overgeneralization to say substance abusers live only for the moment, there is some truth to this statement for some consumers. Most people would readily choose the euphoria associated with some street drugs over the side effects that may result from taking certain psychotropic medications. Treatment professionals have to sell the consumer on giving up the immediate pleasure and accepting some side effects. They have to show the consumer how, in the long run, he will be better off taking the medications rather than using alcohol and other drugs, and how side effects can often be eliminated or managed when he abstains from substance abuse.

Even if a street drug does not have the desired effect, some consumers may keep using it. They may try taking more of it. They may try another supplier. They may even try adding another drug to enhance the effect of the first drug. On the other hand, they may try a psychotropic medication only once. If it does not work fast enough or causes unpleasant side effects, it may be a long time before they agree to try another psychotropic drug.

Murphy's Law of Psychotropic Medication

1. The more beneficial a psychotropic drug could be in the long term, the more easily a consumer will abandon it in the short term—especially if its positive effects are not immediately felt.

2. If a consumer has a question about psychotropic medications, the opinion of the Rhodes scholar, board-certified psychiatrist will hold less weight than that of the neighbor who "knows about these things" through personal experience or the experience of a distant cousin who once took psychotropic drugs.

People diagnosed with a mental illness may blame many of their current and past problems on psychotropic medication. A consumer who two days ago took half his prescribed daily dose of lithium may blame a night of profuse vomiting on the lithium—not on the fifth of liquor he drank. He may find nothing appealing about psychotropic medications.

There is no status in taking Haldol. No rock stars or rap stars hawk Prozac in contrast to alcohol. These drugs are not associated with "special times with good friends." In advertising, alcohol is connected to sexy young men and women, mountain streams, bowling, and an irresistibility to the opposite sex. Most illegal drugs have a street myth about their potency as an aphrodisiac, consciousness expander, tranquilizer, or energizer. At any pick-up basketball game, people wear shirts, shorts, hats, and tennis shoes emblazoned with the name of a malt beverage. Psychotropic medications, on the other hand, carry a stigma. So nobody wears a sweatband or T-shirt emblazoned with "Lithium" or "Prolixin."

TV and movies often portray people on psychotropic medications as not being "quite right." They are often the foil for characters using alcohol who are too often portrayed as "cool" or "bad." Alcohol and other drugs are much more likely to be used to deal with problems than psychotropic medications or self-help groups. On TV the hero gets blind drunk after some cinematic tragedy. Rarely does the star knock back a couple of Thorazines on the way to a Twelve Step meeting.

Despite these misperceptions, consumers can still be sold on abstinence from chemicals and compliance with medications. Several steps should be taken to do this effectively. It is best to start with the basics. What do consumers want; what do they hope to avoid?

What does she want?
Consumers have all the needs of the general population plus needs specific to their mental illness. Start with food. If the consumer was not spending so much on drugs and alcohol, would she eat better?

What benefits could she expect from eating better? She may have an ulcer that she never mentioned. She may not be honest about the physical problems she is experiencing from malnutrition. Whatever the case, it can be amazing how much of a difference something as basic as food can make.

Food is also a good way to attract people who resist treatment (Weiner and Wallen 1988). So many consumers are malnourished that a hot meal, even when served during "that drug and alcohol group," is difficult to resist. For some consumers, it is the only hot meal they will eat that week. It may seem like buying someone's attention, but it is a reasonable bargain: "Listen to this group and we can share a meal. Even if you disregard everything said, you will have heard it and we will have shared a meal."

Some clinics hold regular recovery support lunches. Consumers commit to attending the same luncheon every week no matter what their status in recovery. Each meal celebrates the positive. Consumers list on a chalkboard what they have done in the past week that has helped them stay clean and sober. They list what they hope to do better in the coming week and how long they have been clean. The consumer who has sobered up just long enough to attend that group is applauded for being there. As her sole effort towards recovery, she may write "lunch today" or "sober for six hours." She is applauded for her half day of clean time, offered suggestions, and encouraged to attend other groups in the coming week. Most important, she shares a meal with people who support her.

A hot meal, a positive respite, and a little applause go a long way in helping people deal with early recovery.

What does he hope to avoid?

Keep in mind the AA and NA slogan *Sick and tired of being sick and tired.* What most annoys or scares consumers about their substance abuse and mental illness? For some it is being out of control. For others it is a physical problem, being homeless, or becoming incarcerated.

Many consumers ignore the need for abstinence through a cognitive reversal. The consumer changes his initial assessment of a negative event from, "That almost killed me. I better stop using" to, "I can use all I want because if that didn't kill me, nothing will!" That is why it is important to catch him as soon as possible after substance abuse causes a negative event. If possible, visit a hospitalized patient early the next day or as soon as he is psychiatrically stable. Do not give him time to rationalize away the need to quit using substances. It is easier to sell people life insurance when they are having chest pains.

A consumer who abuses substances may only appear to have stable housing. Several questions need to be asked. Have friends, family, and outside agencies kept him from becoming homeless? How long before he drinks and drugs his way into the homeless shelter? Help him assess when the goodwill of others will dry up and he will be on the street. It may help to show the consumer a homeless shelter. Few shelters offer the amenities of home. Most require residents to leave during the day. Explore with him the idea of having nowhere to *be*. Sell him on avoiding the streets by hanging on to the housing he has. The essential message is that nothing is free; you have to work to hold on to what you have.

If he is already on the street, help him see what role mental illness and/or substance abuse played in landing him in the great outdoors with winter approaching. Too often the "system" rushes in to rescue a consumer before it addresses the reason he needs to be rescued in the first place. Convince him that stable housing is tied to abstinence from chemicals and negotiated compliance with psychotropic medications.

For the recovering consumer, the thought of taking less medication without experiencing an increase in symptoms can be very motivating. The consumer is often told that if he stays off drugs and alcohol long enough, he may have fewer psychiatric symptoms. Consequently, he may have less need for medications, and the psychiatrist will be able to taper psychotropic medications. But before the medications are tapered, help him identify symptoms of decompensation. Agree that if any of these symptoms appear, no further medication reductions will be made until the symptoms remit.

What if she likes her drugs better?

Sometimes a consumer will argue that there is no difference between taking a street drug and taking psychotropic medication. Some will even argue that street drugs and alcohol are better because they do not require a prescription. Try to sell the consumer on the idea that prescribed medications have numerous advantages over nonprescribed drugs. Start with a comparison of getting medication from a physician and buying alcohol and other drugs.

- A consumer can get street drugs whether she needs them or not. No drug dealer has ever told her, "You don't need that. A good night's sleep and some exercise, and you'll feel much better."
- A good physician will not prescribe a medication that is not beneficial to a consumer when weighed against the risks involved in taking it. A dealer will sell cocaine whether the consumer has a weak heart or not.
- The dealer is not interested in helping the consumer taper off the drug. In fact, the more dependent the consumer is on the drug, the better it is for the dealer. Drug dependency is not the dealer's problem. (Few dealers follow a "minimal dose" policy.)
- Changes in personality do not concern the bartender or the drug dealer. If the consumer's mood fails to improve in six weeks, no dealer will lose any sleep over it. As long as the consumer can pay, she can obtain whatever drugs she wants—no matter how they affect her, her family or friends. On the other hand, a good physician will monitor the consumer's mental functioning to see if prescribed medications are working. The physician will note any change in mood, behavior, or thinking, and look for signs of improvement or deterioration due to the medication. Imagine a drug dealer saying, "You look a

little tired—perhaps we should lower your evening dose by ten milligrams."

- Drug dealers are not trained to recognize the physical problems that can result from substance use. Physicians, on the other hand, are trained to look for complications resulting from the medications they prescribe. A physician who prescribes lithium will order regular tests of liver, thyroid, and kidney functioning to make sure it is safe for the consumer to continue taking the medication.

- With prescribed medications, the consumer knows she is getting exactly what was prescribed. The pharmacist will not cut psychotropic medications with baby laxatives or spray them with herbicides. A pharmacist is much more likely than the dealer to make sure it is safe for her to take two different drugs together. Few dealers attach warning labels to their wares that say, "do not mix with alcohol" or "do not operate heavy machinery." Drugs far less sedating than alcohol carry just such a warning.

- Aside from the benzodiazepines, most drugs prescribed for mental illness are far less addicting than the drugs sold by a dealer. Withdrawal from psychotropic medications tends to be very benign. They afford little potential for abuse, provide no immediate "high," and their effect is subtle.

- Unlike street drugs, very few people party with psychotropic medications. Consumers have probably never attended a "lithium bash" or have been served lithium citrate or Trilafon with dinner.

- Prescribed drugs that *can* be abused (such as benzodiazepines like Ativan) still offer some measure of control because they are prescribed. Of course, if benzodiazepines are deemed necessary to treatment, it is critical that a doctor say "when."

Some Twelve Step group members and professionals will not accept the split between street drugs and prescribed medications. Try to provide them with the pertinent information. Whether they choose to believe there is any difference is beyond your control. On the other hand, many people comply with medications once they know the differences.

Intervening with consumers and families

Sometimes people in the consumer's life will not believe that he needs psychiatric treatment. They may be very vocal about their opinions:

- "He only acts like this when he uses cocaine."
- "You people think everyone is crazy."
- "You're not really clean while you take those pills."
- "He has a drug problem and you want to give him more drugs?"

Tell these people they may be right. If the consumer does not have an independent mental illness, the psychiatric symptoms should abate with abstinence from alcohol and other drugs. Help him get clean and sober. Agree with the physician to taper psychotropic medications. If substance abuse is the only problem, then psychotropic medications should not be needed with extended recovery. If he abstains from substances and still experiences psychiatric symptoms, it will be clear that he has a mental illness as well as a substance abuse problem. Simply ask friends and family to work with treatment until the diagnosis becomes clearer.

Celebrating small victories

Recovery from mental illness and substance abuse can be very difficult. Treatment should give the consumer hope and help her keep sight of the happier, more stable life that may appear to be out of reach. You need to celebrate each tiny step along the way. If she cannot remember the last time she had twelve hours of clean time, then twelve hours is well worth celebrating. So are clean clothes, having someone sit next to her on the bus, not being hospitalized, and being able to sit through ten minutes of a community NA meeting. Celebrate each step and point out that the next step may, therefore, be a little easier.

Sell consumers on a different view of the past. One of the best ways to do this is through a *timeline* that charts the role substances have played in their lives (see chapter 9). Expect consumers to resist believing that substance abuse has hurt them. Remember, when you talk about someone's drug of choice, you talk about her mother, lover, world, and self. She may find it hard to believe that something that once made her feel so good and that she holds so dear could be at the root of her instability and unhappiness. She may selectively remember binges as "good times." Even inaccurate memories may be treasured.

Success is the best salesperson. If at all possible, consumers should be introduced to others who are abstaining from substances and are stable in recovery from their mental illness. The more similar the two are, the better. One of the best ways to enhance treatment is to introduce consumers to a recovering consumer who has been through the mill of psychiatric hospitalizations, jail sentences, and substance abuse treatments. Let this person's success be the strongest argument.

Whenever possible, hire consumers stable in recovery from both illnesses to work in your clinic. It shows that recovery is not only possible but also that the hard lessons of addiction and mental illness can help others.

CASE ILLUSTRATION 3: SUCCESS SELLS

Rachel was referred to treatment after being arrested for assault. She was intoxicated at the time of arrest, and the judge agreed to hold the sentence in abeyance while she attended appropriate treatment. In the past Rachel had made similar arrangements, knowing that most drug and alcohol rehabilitation centers would not accept her because of her history of mental illness. If they did accept her, they would not keep her because of her odd behavior and psychiatric symptoms. She would be transferred to a local psychiatric hospital where her symptoms would quickly remit and she would be released. She had become very adept at scamming the system.

Rachel was less than thrilled to discover on release that she had been referred to an outpatient treatment program and that her counselor would stay in touch with her probation officer (P.O.). (Good P.O.s who maintain contact with outpatient clinics are worth their weight in gold. It goes without saying that outpatient clinicians should stay in contact with P.O.s since P.O.s have far more leverage with consumers than clinicians do.)

On her first day at the clinic, Rachel refused depot medications (long-lasting medications administered by injection) and asked for her prescriptions so that she could vacate the premises posthaste. When reminded that she was in treatment in lieu of going to jail, she became verbally abusive.

After much debate, Rachel reluctantly agreed to attend one treatment group session per day, although she refused to participate in the discussion. For several weeks Rachel sat in groups but said nothing. During this time she met several women who had been addicted and psychotic, but had stabilized on very minimal doses of psychotropic medication.

Rachel's charts were reviewed and a timeline was written. She was living at a homeless shelter at this time. Two random urine drug screens were taken each week. When asked what she hoped to achieve in treatment, she said she wanted to "get out of here and be left alone." Staff readily agreed to these two goals on the condition that she feel better and have somewhere to go.

The next day a consumer in recovery showed Rachel his supported-housing apartment. He told her that his only clinical requirement to live there was to meet with a housing counselor once a week. He also told her that while he spent a lot of his time at meetings, it was nice to have a place where he could be alone and not have to answer to anyone. He had found the right marketing tools for Rachel.

That afternoon Rachel demanded that she be given a supported-housing apartment. Staff refused to do so immediately, pointing out that those apartments were for people actively pursuing recovery and stability. An agreement was hammered out with Rachel and her probation officer whereby she agreed to attend all the appropriate treatment and self-help groups. This included two groups per day at the outpatient clinic and community AA and NA meetings. It was also agreed that if she dropped out of treatment, the clinic would immediately notify her probation officer who would recommend she serve the rest of her jail sentence.

For six months she attended treatment sessions regularly but rarely participated. Rachel said almost nothing during a review of her timeline. She seemed interested in nothing but maintaining her apartment. She ate treatment group meals in silence.

At the end of six months Rachel had four months of continuous sobriety. Although she refused to attend any more meetings at the clinic, except for a Twelve Step meeting for mentally ill substance abusers run by consumers, she readily agreed to random drug screens.

The Point Is . . .

1. It is often the basics, like shelter, that attract people to treatment.

2. It is more important that someone agrees to a drug screen and attends meetings on her own than it is for her to cooperate with staff. If you can verify a consumer is abstaining from a previously abused substance, does it matter where she learns how? You will be the first to know if she is not taking care of her mental illness and substance abuse problem.

3. Other consumers are your best salespeople. It was the consumer with the supervised apartment who sparked Rachel's interest in treatment. He was not selling anything different from the treatment staff; he was just more believable. Whom do you trust more—the guy who's trying to sell you the car or the woman down the block who drives one?

Becoming a treatment team player

Most consumers need to be treated by a team rather than an individual. The team might include a clinician, a physician, a residential care worker, a social rehabilitation expert, a vocational specialist, the consumer's sponsor, and anyone else concerned. The more people involved, the better. Society may be telling the consumer that psychotropic medications are bad and that alcohol and other drugs are good. The treatment team may need many people to send an alternative message. To do so effectively they should be united.

The ideal would be for everyone on the team to share the same goals and beliefs. This may not happen. The treatment team members have different educational experiences, cultural backgrounds, experiences with the consumer, and expectations of the role they play in treatment.

Everybody has a unique style of dealing with consumers. For example, if a consumer relapses, some treatment team members may argue with him. Others will try to reason with him, while still others will try to be more supportive. When people with different approaches work together on difficult problems, disagreements happen. Expect this, but also expect the team to develop a sense of purpose as consumers once thought to be hopeless regain their sanity and serenity.

Substance abuse brings up professionals' own issues regarding intoxication, abuse, and control. Sadly most of us have been touched in one way or another by substance abuse. A treatment team member in recovery may have a different outlook than another treatment team member whose religion forbade the use of mind-altering substances.

Team members may also disagree about how responsible the consumer is for his actions. Most would agree that when people abuse substances their thinking and judgment are impaired, yet they are still responsible for their actions. If they have an automobile accident while drunk, they are still responsible, because presumably they knew the consequences when they began using alcohol and other drugs.

What about the person who is feeling fine and quits taking medications? Is he responsible for his actions while his thinking and judgment are clouded by mental illness? What if his thinking never completely clears? Is he then only partially responsible for his actions? There will always be judgment calls regarding how responsible the consumer is for whatever happens to him. There may be disagreement among the treatment team as to the consumer's and other treatment team members' judgment. This does not have to be divisive.

The treatment team need only agree on two key issues. One, they must agree to have an ongoing dialogue. The easiest way to sabotage treatment is to have a fragmented treatment team with members not sharing information. Two, the treatment team must also agree that abstinence and medication compliance are two primary goals. If one member of the treatment team tells the consumer he need not take his medication, then there is little chance that any other member of the team will be able to convince the consumer otherwise. This also holds true if a member of the treatment team tells him abstinence from abused substances is not important.

Agree that the consumer needs to get off substances and on a negotiated level of medications. Everything else about treatment should be open for discussion.

Ideally, the team works for the consumer, but the consumer should be the leader and driving force of the treatment team. Unfortunately, some consumers may consider the treatment team an adversary. These consumers use a number of techniques to sabotage treatment.

The truly oppositional consumer will consciously or unconsciously exploit all of the differences of opinion mentioned above. He will find new and exciting ways to play the treatment team members against each other. If allowed to, he ensures that treatment grinds to a halt while the team argues about trivial matters. Recognize this and agree to keep working with the consumer and other team members *no matter what.*

Quality assurance: How well are professionals "selling" recovery?

The consumer may not reach the ultimate goals of abstinence and stability for a long time. This does not mean she is not getting healthier as she moves towards these goals. Nor does it mean that the treatment program is not working. Rather it signals a need to reassess how well the consumer is doing and how much effort is being made to help her.

First, assess what the treatment program offers the consumer to help her recover from both illnesses. The consumer has a tough row to hoe—what has been done to make it easier for her to overcome mental illness and substance abuse?

List the services provided. Writing down what is actually done is a good way to concretely examine the strengths and weaknesses of the treatment program. Two agencies may both say they help consumers use Twelve Step programs. However, when they list what they do, one agency may write that they only provide lists of Twelve Step meetings. The other agency may take consumers to meetings, hold "practice" meetings (see chapter 11), and actively seek volunteers from the recovering community to talk to consumers.

How accessible are the services? Can consumers quickly and easily get to treatment? What good is it to give a consumer recovery literature that she cannot read? On the other hand, providing large-print copies and reviewing with her everything she has read is truly doing something.

Assess improvement in the treatment program. Have any new treatment groups been added? Are people keeping more appointments? Are families satisfied with the services consumers receive? Are more consumers attending self-help meetings? Has the program attracted any new consumers? Have staff members gotten any more training on mental illness or substance abuse? How is the program better today than yesterday?

It would be wonderful if everyone in treatment quit abusing alcohol and other drugs the first day in your clinic. It may not happen. It is more realistic to assess a consumer's progress toward abstinence and stability. Ask what effect the treatment program has on participants. Are more people admitting they have a problem? Are consumers staying away from substances longer? Are they taking psychotropic medications as prescribed? Are they having fewer side effects from the medications? Are consumers being hospitalized less often? Is there an increase in family involvement? The question is whether the consumer is any closer to her goals while in treatment. Really giant steps may appear to cover only small distances.

Remember, too, that these suggestions are everything that can and should be done under *ideal* circumstances. The program may have limited time or resources. Be fair. If the treatment program does not have the resources to expand what it does, ask yourself, have I done the best I can with the resources available to me?

The Point Is . . .

Remember to celebrate your own small steps.

———≫●≪———

CHAPTER 3

Assessment

A day in the life

There are many methods for gathering information about consumers, their use of alcohol and other drugs, and their mental health problems. Clinicians will want to tailor assessment techniques to fit the consumers they serve. The following guidelines should make the assessment process a little easier.

Gather information from as many sources as possible, but evaluate each source. For example, an uncle who insists a consumer does not have a drinking problem as he finishes his 10 A.M. beer may not be the most reliable source. A recovering family member may provide a more accurate picture of the consumer's alcohol and other drug use. Do not assume information from medical, mental health, or social service professionals is completely accurate either. Read medical reports with a wary eye—many professionals hesitate to diagnose substance abuse or do not know how to do so.

Assessment should be more than finding out which diagnostic criterion a person meets. Try to find out what it is like for each consumer to have psychiatric symptoms. Knowing that someone experiences auditory hallucinations indicates he may have schizophrenia. Knowing the person feels "tortured by female voices" provides a better idea of what his day is like and why he is uncomfortable in coed groups.

Conduct assessments matter-of-factly but with some concern. It is important not to be too clinical or too easily amazed by consumers' stories. When talking about the addict's chemical of choice, expect some denial, evasiveness, hostility, and defensiveness. Expect consumers to say things like

- "I got it right off the plane from Columbia."
- "I have two beers on New Year's Eve every leap year."
- "You want to take away my right to buy cocaine?"
- "You never got drunk at a Christmas party?"
- "It's only beer. I don't do drugs, so what's the big deal?"
- "I smoke a joint to help me deal with the voices. If you had voices, you might smoke a little too."
- "All my friends get high. What do you expect me to do?"

Try not to let the consumer's minimization and rationalization throw you off balance. Keep gathering information. Often you will discover some bit of information that sheds light on what is already known. If a consumer says he abstained from alcohol and other drugs for months at a time, find out what helped him stay clean. He may have been attending a treatment program that helped him maintain his sobriety. Or he may have been in the state hospital and unable to obtain alcohol and other drugs.

Note the emotion and the response to questions without comment. On the other hand, it is important not to drone on in a monotone with questions as a consumer describes very painful segments of his life. He may want the answer to the basic question: "Can you help me get over all these problems?" If the counselor cannot put down the clipboard long enough to express some empathy, the consumer may conclude that he can expect no help.

Spend as much time as possible learning how the consumer's life sounds, tastes, looks, and feels. What weighs heaviest, what lifts his burden, what makes him soar? Where does he live in his world? Is he an actor or is he acted upon? What rules and roles does he follow and who makes them? What surprises him; what does he expect? Whom can he trust?

Spend as much time as you can with the consumer. If at all possible, make home visits. Talk to the consumer's friends and family. Do not simply see the trail he is traveling—walk beside him and ask him what he sees. Try to see the terrain through his eyes without losing sight of your own vision. You may see an SSI (Supplemental Security Income) check that could be stretched over the whole month. He sees thirty days of scrimping after blandness: bland food, bland TV, bland people at the clinic, bland life. You see a weekend binge that may exhaust his resources and threaten his health and sanity. He sees an oasis of euphoria in a desert of drab. You see long-term, life-threatening problems. He sees short-term relief.

Try to see why he does things. When a consumer says he cannot take a ten-minute bus ride, is it because he is agoraphobic, malingering, paranoid, lazy, independent and assertive, or just not interested? Is his behavior tied to his delusional system or dictated by an addiction? The "why" is at least as important as the "what." Never assume to know why. If they're not careful, clinicians tend to personalize, assuming the consumer is angry with them or not interested in treatment.

During assessment, keep in mind the AA and NA slogan *People, places, and things.* What people, places, and things are associated with his chemical use? Look for patterns to his substance use. Sometimes the patterns are defined by your vision. It may be plain to you that the consumer gets high every time he visits a certain friend. Sometimes the pattern is in the consumer's vision, such as using marijuana instead of lithium because he now sees "the reason for it all" and with marijuana he just knows he will find what he needs.

Know when a consumer will be getting money from any source. This is vital to knowing which days, months, and seasons are high-risk times for the consumer's substance abuse. The consumer with a "check day" habit is common. Other consumers may have a tougher time staying clean around painful anniversaries, such as the death of a loved one. This is not limited to the actual day of the anniversary. A consumer who in mid-October found his father dying from gaping knife wounds may became more symptomatic as the air grows crisper and the leaves change colors. The red of fall foliage can evoke vivid recollections that render him symptomatic and ripe for relapse to both substance abuse and mental illness. Less dramatic is the woman who drank on each of her four children's birthdays.

An increase in psychiatric symptoms and substance abuse may be cyclical. It is not uncommon for consumers to become more depressed in the winter. This can contribute to substance abuse. Some are more prone to use just before or after they receive an injection of depot medications. Female consumers' use of alcohol and other drugs may be related to menstrual cycles.

Trust me, I'm wearing white

A trip to the dentist can provide a small insight into what life is like for some consumers. Imagine your dentist works for a chain of dental offices that caters to chickens. They pride themselves on providing pain-free dentistry. In all the time you have visited this dentist, he has only caused a twinge of pain, and that was when the Novocain needle hit a nerve. He is a very likable man with a quick wit. There is an easy camaraderie among his staff, and he is always thorough and professional.

You lounge calmly in the chair until he looms over you with the needle in his hand. Suddenly, you notice the beadiness of his eyes. Was that a tremble in his hands? Was he afraid, eager, or withdrawing from some mind-altering drug? His diplomas are hung on the far wall, impossible to read from the prone and helpless position in his strange chair. Your mind races through past episodes of *America's Most Wanted.* That guy in Texas who killed his wife—what would he look like in a beard? And that time he hit the nerve—had he been a little too apologetic?

All these thoughts race through your mind in a split second and are gone. You see these thoughts for what they are, spastic distortions of panic. Some consumers are not always able to do this—their mental illness may interfere with their ability to identify real from imagined danger. Or they may find small amounts of stress intolerable. Feelings that most people dismiss may greatly upset someone coping with a mental illness. They may have a difficult time trusting people who say they want to help.

A clinician may say, "My name is Sue. I'm the outpatient evaluation nurse here at County Memorial. I just need to ask you a few questions, okay?" "Okay" is said in that singsong voice that is supposed to convey harmless caring. Sue believes that her status as a nurse should convince her patient of her ability and professionalism. When she says, "County Memorial," she hears, "well-run, well-regulated, teaching and research hospital." But that is not what the consumer hears.

The last nurse from County Memorial this consumer encountered used that same singsong voice. But that nurse said, "This isn't going to hurt a bit unless you keep squirming." He had said it through clenched teeth. What the four police officers holding the consumer down said was considerably more foul. This nurse had also wanted to ask a few questions and apparently had not been satisfied with the answers. The consumer has a frightening sense of déjà vu as she answers Sue's questions.

This consumer knows nothing of County's venerable reputation. She knows that friends call it "County in Memorium." She also knows that these are the same people who brought her forced medications, seclusion, and a muttering, mooching, intrusive roommate.

Sue should not be surprised that this consumer is less than eager to answer her questions. She should not interpret it as resistance. It is her job to help the consumer overcome her reservations. It is her job to enable the consumer to hear what she thought she was saying. It takes time and a whole lot of patience.

Gather whatever information is available, verify as much as possible, and build a relationship with the consumer. Going into the first interview without expecting to get all the information eliminates a lot of frustration. Always keep in mind that relationship-building is essential to good treatment. Time spent with a consumer is never wasted. If after the first interview she is slightly less suspicious, or if any new information came to light, the interview was a success.

It never ends, but it always changes
Assessing the consumer can be very frustrating for clinicians who like to use clean, uncomplicated information to reach a clear diagnosis. When a consumer is actively using substances, it may not be clear what or how much he is using. It may not be clear if his psychiatric symptoms are from drug abuse, mental illness, both, or from an undiscovered physical ailment. It may not be clear how severe the mental illness symptoms would be if he abstained from drug use. It may not be clear if his use of substances is an attempt to self-medicate or why he needs medication.

Many factors complicate the diagnosis as manifestations of the mental illness change over time. Many illnesses run in cycles, such as seasonal depressions. Others have a chronic course—it may seem that the consumer is always symptomatic. Still others are episodic, with acute flare-ups of symptoms that are years apart. How someone looks on any particular day is not a good indicator of his overall well-being.

Clinicians may never be sure a consumer takes psychotropic medications as prescribed. It is a big mistake to rule out an illness because drugs typically prescribed for that illness have proven ineffective. Too often a consumer will take psychotropic medications the way he takes street drugs: in larger quantities than suggested when in acute stress, or to get an immediate high. The fact that lithium does not stop his mood swings does not indicate that he does not suffer from bipolar disorder. It may indicate that he is taking lithium only when he feels bad. If after ten minutes he does not feel a "buzz," he may decide that lithium does not work or that he needs to take more than the doctor recommended. Since he has not taken any all week, there are plenty of pills left for him to "catch up."

Without accurate drug screens it is difficult to know what psychiatric symptoms are tied to substance use. Consumers often change their drug of choice or try new combinations of street drugs. Depending on the amount of a chemical in his body, a consumer may display a variety of psychiatric symptoms. If he smokes crack, he may appear manic or depressed, depending on how much he used and where he is in the cycle of crack abuse. Withdrawal from alcohol and other drugs can produce symptoms that mimic mental illness. Symptoms of mental illness can be triggered by substance abuse and withdrawal.

Once a consumer acquires clean time, his whole life may change. Beginning recovery from substance abuse with a mental illness has been likened to waking up from a coma, outside, in the dead of winter. A common complaint is "I got sober for this?" As people come to terms with their situation, their mood may fluctuate rapidly. The problems and symptoms that have been anesthetized often wake up with a foul temper. Periods of acute depression and panic are common. The stress of early recovery may exacerbate schizophrenic symptoms. The diagnostic picture may change weekly as people used to running from their feelings turn to face them. Be as supportive as possible, celebrating each positive step.

Early recovery can also be a time of great joy. A consumer may be amazed at the sense of mastery obtained by meeting new challenges without chemicals. He can be buoyed by the thought that if he can stay clean for a day, perhaps he can stay clean for a week. After a week, a month, and several months have passed, he may start to suspect that anything is possible.

The greatest blessing of abstinence from alcohol and other drugs is that there are often fewer psychiatric symptoms to report. For example, suppose a consumer uses substances to deaden psychiatric symptoms. But then using alcohol and other drugs worsens his symptoms, creating the desire for more drugs. One consumer, for example, reported that his addiction developed from attempts to "party" with his voices: "They used to be fun to drink with, but they started getting vicious." Before he quit drinking, the voices were telling him to kill himself. Abstinence from alcohol lessened the severity of his psychiatric symptoms, enabling him to break this vicious cycle.

Who would lie to someone wearing white?
Corroborate information whenever possible. Like most substance abusers, the consumer is prone to denial, a form of delusion. As such, it is an unconscious defense mechanism that protects her from seeing how substance abuse has hurt her. It allows the alcoholic to say, "It's not me or the booze, it's _____" and then fill in the blank with something beyond her control that will cast her in a sympathetic light.

Denial is not lying. It is a defense that saves the consumer from realizing she has a problem with substances and that she may have to abstain from them. Denial enables her to see her substance abuse as still being under control long after she has lost control.

CASE ILLUSTRATION 4: DENIAL BY DEFINITION

Andrew, a recovering alcoholic, shows how someone who drinks four days per week sees himself as a "weekend drinker."

In my mind alcoholics drank every day, while social drinkers drank on weekends. (And special occasions like Arbor Day and Robert Goddard's birthday.) I decided that I would only drink on weekends. From Friday to Sunday I stayed drunk. Still I felt empty and had a sense of foreboding. Monday was my recovery day. On Tuesday I would annoy everyone around me with my "I only drink on weekends, more-chipper-than-thou attitude." Wednesday the blahs set in, and by Thursday I was wishing the weekend would get here already.

> *Not long after I had confined my drinking to weekends—except for attempts to save others from addiction by helping them drink their beer—I was sitting in the TV lounge at school when my roommate walked in.*
>
> *"Don't you have a test to study for?" he asked.*
>
> *"It's not 'til Friday afternoon," I told him.*
>
> *"It is now 12:05 Friday morning," he said. And then it hit me. He was right. It was really Friday.*
>
> *From that time on, I considered Thursday at midnight part of the weekend. And if you're going to drink at midnight, you might as well have a few watching the news at eleven. I got drunk Thursday through Sunday and absolutely, unshakably, and with the deepest of conviction believed I only drank on weekends.*

The Point Is . . .

1. Denial is not lying. It is an unconscious defense mechanism against facing addiction.
2. Denial lives in definitions. The way Andrew defines *weekend* is what allows him to believe that he is a weekend drinker.

A consumer who says she has not used a chemical for six months may have a distorted understanding of abstinence, believing that abstinence means not using illegal drugs like cocaine. "Cocaine is illegal; my problems have been with the legal system," she may say. She believes that since alcohol is legal, it cannot be a problem. She may be drinking a six-pack each day but report no substance use.

Even when asked specifically about alcohol, she may report no use because she differentiates between *alcohol* and *beer*. Beer is often not seen as the *hard stuff,* as somehow being in a different category than wine and liquor. Many adults drink no other alcoholic beverages but beer. And it is one of the few alcoholic beverages that is viewed as a thirst quencher. Some consumers just do not consider beer to be alcohol.

Marijuana, which has been decriminalized in several states, is seen as a "soft" drug in comparison to cocaine or opiates. Many do not consider smoking marijuana a form of drug abuse. One consumer argued that marijuana was "natural" since it grows wild. She said she would take Prolixin when she could be shown a "Prolixin bush." When asked initially about substance use, this woman denied using any substances because she felt marijuana was an "herb" and was not in the same category as alcohol and other "refined" drugs.

The social context that alcohol and other drugs are used in may also dictate how consumers view their use. A consumer who says she has had nothing to drink for six months may believe the six gin and tonics she had at her cousin's wedding reception are not worth mentioning. After all, even her grandmother drank at the reception. She may believe that it would be an insult to the bride and groom not to drink. Many newcomers to Twelve Step programs are shocked to discover that abstinence from alcohol and other drugs includes holidays, birthdays, and special occasions. There is a myth that everyone will use alcohol "at least" at certain events.

Denial can center on a specific chemical. Some consumers will decide one chemical is the "villain" while all others are more or less benign. Abstinence for these consumers means abstinence from that particular chemical. They will often switch to another chemical, extolling its virtues while vilifying their former favorite: "That 'caine was kickin my ass, but weed just makes me mellow." For example, an inpatient stormed out of group when the discussion switched from LSD to alcohol. Prior to leaving she had been open and supportive of other group members, describing LSD as "the worst thing a schizophrenic can do." When reminded that she had arrived at the hospital drunk, she pointed out that this was a "drug group," that she had given up her drugs—LSD and marijuana—and that the group should not waste time talking about something like alcohol that was not a "real" drug.

Even if a consumer accepts the notion that a drug is a drug is a drug, she may get caught up in how much counts as "use" or "abuse." She may set her own limit, and any less she will not count as drug use. If that limit is twenty dollars worth of crack and someone let her hit the crack pipe for free, she may not report any drug use to the clinician—not because she is lying, but because she does not consider it "really using" to smoke less than twenty dollars worth of crack.

The individual decides what constitutes a drug, drug abuse, psychiatric symptoms, and abstinence. Denial occurs when the person's interpretations differ from reality. This difference is not due to lying, but to a world view skewed by a mental illness and a strong bias against having to deal with addiction.

Who's kidding who?

Delusions are not lying, but misinterpretations of the outside world caused by brain dysfunctions. Although paranoia is the most common delusion, there are many others. They can greatly color the assessment process. For example, a consumer who has delusions of grandeur may have a difficult time seeing how he could possibly have any problem with substance abuse. In his mind only "lowlifes" drink too much or cannot control their use of street drugs. Someone with the special talents and abilities he believes he possesses will not, in his estimation, become addicted. If asked about problems with substance abuse, he is unlikely to report any. He is much more likely to offer advice for others who do not have his "control" over alcohol and other drugs.

Most delusions start with a faulty premise that is supported by an idiosyncratic interpretation. A consumer may believe that a certain TV commercial means he is to leave his house immediately to avoid disaster (faulty premise). For weeks he leaps from his chair and flies through the door each time this commercial is aired. Nothing disastrous happens. He concludes that leaving his house has saved him (idiosyncratic interpretation). His belief in this delusion is set in concrete. It would be frustrating at best to argue with this consumer about the significance of the commercial. In his mind the premise that the commercial is a warning has been validated by his escapes from disaster. "I'm still alive—isn't that proof enough?" he asks.

That is not to say that every utterance from a consumer is denial or a delusion. Sometimes consumers simply lie. A consumer will look you right in the eye, hope you do not smell the booze on his breath or the smoke on his clothes, and lie about his substance abuse.

"Have you used alcohol in the past week?" you ask. "Absolutely not," he answers. "I'm on medication that doesn't mix with booze and hard drugs scare me. Besides, they don't allow us to stay at the group home if we use."

Most consumers know what you, the treatment professional, want to hear. Some want to keep using alcohol and other drugs. They have a fair belief that no professional is going to support their substance abuse. They don't like being confronted about it. Why not say whatever will keep people from dealing with their substance abuse?

A consumer may have *realistic* fears about the treatment team's response to his substance abuse. Will the clinician refuse to see him for counseling sessions? Will the doctor refuse to prescribe medications, taking him off those benzodiazepines he likes so much? Will he lose his bed at the residential rehabilitation center? Will the volunteer quit stopping by?

He may also have *unrealistic* fears that are part of his mental illness. Will he be committed to the psychiatric hospital for using? Will you tell the authorities? Why do people want to know about his use of alcohol and other drugs?

From the consumer's point of view, there may be very little incentive to be honest about substance abuse when lying keeps the treatment team from interfering with his chemical use. Why tell the truth when a lie will keep you off his back? Is it not enough that he has to answer all these questions about mental illness? Sadly, he may know from past experience that many mental health professionals are not all that interested in his chemical use. And he believes these professionals can be put off much more easily than those persistently annoying counselors at the drug and alcohol center. If he is the least bit insightful, he may know that many mental health professionals are uncomfortable talking about drug and alcohol issues. Why bring them up in the first place? In short, expect some consumers to lie about their chemical use.

Reassure the consumer that he can be truthful about his use of alcohol and other drugs. It helps to tell consumers why you're asking about their substance abuse. Assure them that the treatment team isn't looking for an excuse to "put them away." Make sure they know there is a good clinical reason for wanting to know about their use of alcohol and other drugs.

Tell consumers that the team cannot provide adequate treatment without adequate information. Without accurate information there is no way to know which medications work and which do not work. You will not know what causes certain psychiatric symptoms, and some symptoms may be treated with medication that would disappear with abstinence from alcohol and other drugs.

Tell consumers you are worried about them. If they use alcohol and other drugs while on medication, they may experience more side effects. Substance abuse may lower the effectiveness of psychotropic medication. Seizure, strokes, changes in blood pressure, increased anxiety, and depressive symptoms are also more likely to occur.

The myth of a primary diagnosis

Although the mental health treatment system is changing, too much effort goes into deciding which diagnosis is primary. Some professionals assume that if the "primary problem" is treated, the "other problem" will fall into place. For example, many mental health clinicians still believe that if the depression is primary, treating the depression will eliminate the "need" to use drugs. On the other hand, drug and alcohol professionals may argue that once the substance is removed and recovery begun, many social and emotional problems will diminish. This may be true for people coping with one illness, but it is not always true for consumers coping with both. Some people have two problems that are intertwined but separate entities. Trying to decide which is primary does little to benefit them.

If a diabetic becomes addicted to cocaine, is her diabetes cured when she begins recovery? Absolutely not. She still has an imbalance in her body that affects her mood and health. If someone is depressed for years before she picks up that first drink, will recovery automatically cure her depression? Absolutely not, because she may still have a bodily imbalance that affects her mood and health.

Some professionals will insist on choosing a primary illness. The temptation after deciding which is primary is to send the consumer to a clinic that specializes in that problem. Consider the mistakes that can be made when searching for a primary diagnosis and appropriate treatment.

CASE ILLUSTRATION 5: IS HALF A DIAGNOSIS
REALLY BETTER THAN NONE?

Sam is crying when he arrives at the emergency room of a local hospital. It is January 2. He is grossly intoxicated and complains of a severely depressed mood with suicidal thoughts. He tells the resident on duty that he drinks only on special occasions. The resident, suffering through the aftermath of his own excesses, feels a sad camaraderie with Sam. In Sam's chart he writes "R/O [rule out] alcohol abuse" and presses on with the interview. The resident discovers that Sam has made several serious suicide attempts in the past ten years, usually following bouts of deep depression. He is struck by Sam's flat presentation of an existence that is bleak in the extreme.

"No wonder he got drunk," the resident says to himself. "Another year like last year just beginning." He suspects the patient is drinking more than he lets on but does not ask him any more questions about substance abuse. The resident has had two hours of training about addiction and knows more about the plague.

Looking through the chart, he discovers that Sam has tried the antidepressants Elavil, Norpramin, and Desyrel. None has significantly lifted his depression. The records do not mention how much Sam was drinking while on these medications.

The resident concludes that Sam is suffering from major depression. With great enthusiasm he explains that new antidepressants have been marketed since his last bout of depression. He writes orders for Prozac and sends Sam to the inpatient unit where after several alcohol-free weeks, he feels remarkably better. Sam celebrates his release from the hospital with several pitchers of draft beer at a bar two blocks from the hospital. He believes they know what is wrong with him and they now have something that works for his primary problem, depression.

After a month of heavy drinking, Sam becomes severely depressed. The outpatient clinician, who has never seen this consumer sober, suspects that Sam is an alcoholic. She refers him to a drug and alcohol rehabilitation center where Sam discovers that many alcoholics are depressed—they are depressed while they are drinking and are often depressed early in recovery. At Alcoholics Anonymous meetings at the rehabilitation center he discovers a number of people who threw their pills away and lived happily ever after. He becomes more than a little angry with the mental health system for giving him medications while ignoring his alcoholism.

Now that he has been "correctly" diagnosed, he is told he will be able to use the tools of the program to deal with his primary problem, alcoholism.

Initially his depression clears, but two months out of the rehabilitation center his depression returns with a vengeance. Some Alcoholics Anonymous members tell him to attend more meetings. They chide him about self-pity and advise him to get involved with someone worse off than himself. He ignores the advice of people in Alcoholics Anonymous who tell him to go back to his doctor and abstain from alcohol.

Three months after he is discharged from the rehabilitation center, he is homeless and depressed. He spends much of his time panhandling his next drink and wondering what is his "primary" problem.

The Point Is . . .

1. Assessment should start with the understanding that people can have many problems that need attention at the same time, in the same place, by the same people.

2. If you only diagnose and treat the mental illness, you may tacitly endorse substance abuse. There is an old joke in AA that "drunks who get years of analysis become well-adjusted drunks." The chronically mentally ill rarely make it that far while they are using alcohol and other drugs.

3. If you only treat substance abuse, the consumer may have difficulty staying clean and using Twelve Step programs. The quality of her recovery may be so poor that she feels compelled to use alcohol and other drugs again.

CHAPTER 4

—————

ATTITUDES OF PROFESSIONALS

Attitudes and mistaken beliefs about consumers, mental illness, and substance abuse can interfere with providing the best treatment possible. What follows is a general guide for examining your attitudes about mental illness and substance abuse. Remember, your attitude may be the most important component of treatment that you control.

Selling long-term solutions

Treating the consumer requires the ability to sell the consumer on long-term solutions. In the long term the treatment team is selling stability and serenity, fewer psychiatric symptoms, less psychotropic medication, fewer medication side effects, fewer hospitalizations, fewer legal problems, and more lasting personal relationships. The team would seem to have just what every consumer wants. Why then is it so hard to "sell" recovery from either disorder? The problem is in the short term.

From the view of the consumer who still loves smoking crack the team is saying, "Forget the fifteen-minute, full-body orgasm; forget the high-status drug that people are willing to kill for; forget fitting in with everyone you know; forget the one thing that you think truly loves you. Take this drug instead: one that requires taking blood levels and blurs your vision; one you couldn't give away if it came with a free meal and fifty dollars in cash."

You need to sell the consumer on the idea that he will be much better off without his drug of choice in the long term. So how do you get past short-term resistance to long-term success? Start with your own attitude.

Provide a consistent and positive message about recovery from mental illness and substance abuse. Celebrate each small victory, and confront the use of alcohol and other drugs. To do this, it helps to be very clear about your own beliefs. *Believe that people can recover from both illnesses.* If you do not believe recovery is possible, you are wasting the consumer's time. Believe this and you can make a world of difference.

Giving up

Too often treatment professionals forget that until someone has amassed months of clean time, the severity of her mental illness is unknown. It is also unknown how much she might gain from Twelve Step programs or other support groups if her mental illness were in remission or improved. She may be hallucinating now, but who knows what she would be like sober and on medications? The beauty of working in this field is that some consumers make miraculous recoveries.

In combination, mental illness and substance abuse may mask the consumer's strengths and abilities. But the moment someone is labeled "hopeless," her potential is buried. Treat the mental illness and substance abuse at the same time and discover how much potential a "hopeless" consumer has. Do not give up, do not paddle away.

CASE ILLUSTRATION 6: HIDDEN POTENTIAL

Mike, a twenty-seven-year-old man with a five-year history of substance abuse, was hospitalized ten times in two years, usually after cocaine binges. Mike carried a diagnosis of "catatonic schizophrenia and substance abuse." In recent years he had been smoking crack "as often as possible." He was extremely thin and had lost two front teeth in a brawl.

Although Mike was not formally labeled "hopeless," few people saw a bright future for him. At his last hospitalization, Mike was told that one of three things might happen to him:

he would die, be committed to a long-term hospitalization, or land in jail. Fearing all three, he began working the first step of Narcotics Anonymous while still hospitalized. Upon discharge he bought a bus pass and began spending all day riding to and from Narcotics Anonymous meetings. Mike also found a sponsor and a home group. In the past two years he has been hospitalized only once—he had a catatonic episode but did not use alcohol and other drugs prior to it.

Mike spent some time working for a residential treatment facility and currently works for a local hospital coleading substance abuse groups. He obtained a graduate equivalency degree and is currently attending college and wants to become a certified addictions counselor.

The Point Is . . .

1. Most people are hospitalized far less often while abstaining from alcohol and other drugs.
2. Mental illness is more easily managed when people abstain from alcohol and other drugs.
3. Someone suffering from psychiatric symptoms who does not pick up the first drink/drug can be greatly admired.
4. After repeated hospitalizations it is easy to lose sight of someone's abilities. Yet, you never know what a consumer is capable of until she is clean of substances and compliant with medications.

Enabling

Enabling can be very addictive. Picture yourself as the only psychiatrist in an outpatient clinic on a Friday afternoon. A colleague has left instructions that if a certain consumer shows up, there are prewritten prescriptions in the top desk drawer. His appointment was for three o'clock. But sure enough, at a quarter to five this consumer lumbers in, opening the door without knocking. He is, according to hidden consensus, the staff members' least favorite. (Liking or disliking consumers is rarely talked about, but it should be!) Whiny and demanding, he has a strong sense of entitlement and an even stronger body odor.

"Where's my 'scripts?" he asks, swaying slightly and slurring his speech. Numerous clinicians have tried a variety of tactics to deal with his attitude and substance abuse. There is no such thing as a brief encounter with him.

Denying him prescriptions now means dealing with his entire enabling family later. They will call you at home. They will call the medical director. They will question your credentials. They will call your boss, his boss, her boss, and the boss of all bosses.

Instead of working with another consumer and her family who are trying diligently to deal with their issues, you will spend Monday talking to the patient advocate, the county monitor, the state administrator, and the regional patient representative. A good friend of the president will call, unofficially of course, to see just what *the* problem is. The paperwork will pile up until you think community mental health is just a scam perpetrated by the lumber industry to create a demand for paper products.

Thinking about this gives you a sick and sinking feeling. Rationalizations spring to mind—he is not your responsibility; he will still be intoxicated whether you confront him or not; he is not worth the hassle. Give him the prescriptions and he will immediately leave. The unpleasant feeling will dissolve before you start your weekend.

You hand him the prescriptions. He turns his head and reaches for them with his arm fully extended. He does not want you to smell his breath. As he walks out the door, you let out a sigh of relief. The tension drains from your body. The sensation might even be described as a "rush."

Part of addiction is trading short-term relief for long-term problems. The addict feels uncomfortable and ingests some of his favorite chemical. The tension or craving eases and he feels rewarded. It is only in the long term that problems develop. Enabling is the mirror image of addiction.

The enabler allowed the consumer to get prescriptions despite being late and drunk. He traded the short-term relief of having the consumer out of the office for several long-term problems. The consumer now knows he can come to the clinic drunk. He knows that late on Friday afternoons staff would rather not deal with him. He knows at least one staff member who does not think his drinking is worth mentioning. And he knows several other consumers who will soon know what he knows.

Check your attitude. If you think enabling will make your job easier, think about a caseload of people who expect you to overlook their substance abuse. It is vital to matter-of-factly confront any use of alcohol and other drugs. You will be amazed at the difference it can make.

Confronting

Some professionals argue that if they confront substance abuse, some consumers will drop out of treatment. The argument seems to be that even if the consumer continues to use alcohol and other drugs, at least she is in treatment. Isn't it better to have contact with her while she is using alcohol and other drugs than to risk having her leave the system completely?

There are several flaws with this argument. One is the assumption that just being associated with a program is beneficial. If the consumer continues using and nobody says anything, she will think her substance abuse is not a problem. She may say to herself, "When my psychiatric symptoms flare up, they get me 'round-the-clock care at the hospital, but when I get drunk nobody says anything." She may decide not to worry about her substance abuse since the treatment professionals are not worried. She may stay in your program under the erroneous assumption that she is getting the appropriate treatment.

Imagine going to your doctor complaining of chest pain. The doctor discovers the chest pain was caused partly by stress and partly by a small tumor. He decides that saying anything about the tumor will be too upsetting. Instead he prescribes painkillers and provides a videotape on stress management.

"If I had told her about the tumor, she would have gone over the edge and not gotten any treatment," the doctor testifies. "By not telling her, I was at least able to help her with the pain and stress." You, of course, die a premature if well-medicated death, but your family gets a nice settlement. The point is that not addressing substance abuse to keep someone in treatment is worse than providing no treatment at all. At least the consumer who is out of treatment knows she is not getting adequate care.

Besides, is there any real treatment going on while the consumer is actively using? The illnesses cannot be treated separately with any hope of success. Someone taking Prozac and participating in cognitive psychotherapy is unlikely to feel any less depressed while she drinks two pints of vodka each day. Who can teach her to manage money if she spends three-fourths of it on marijuana? Worse, is she getting the message that treatment does not work? After all, she took Prozac for six months and was still depressed. Nobody told her that alcohol is worsening her depression. She may think booze is the only thing that makes the depression tolerable. If it was part of the problem somebody would have said something, right?

Surprisingly, she may not leave the program. Threats to terminate treatment are often a bluff. But if the threat gets the treatment professional to back off, then she will use that threat again and again. There is no way of knowing if she means it. She may be a master at getting people to ignore her substance abuse. She may try to make you feel guilty, incompetent, or cruel when you confront her about substance abuse. *Confront her anyway.*

Confronting a consumer does not mean throwing her out of a treatment program. It means calmly stating concerns and making it as difficult as possible for her to use alcohol and other drugs. It means holding her responsible for the consequences of her substance abuse.

Being needed

Shielding the consumer from the consequences of continued substance abuse is a common mistake. The idea is that he may never stop using substances, but at least treatment professionals can stop bad things from happening to him. This is a form of enabling. Part of confronting is allowing the consumer to be uncomfortable when he uses alcohol and other drugs. If he leaves treatment because of some negative event the treatment team could have prevented, that is still his choice to leave. The team has not "done" something bad to him.

Before helping a consumer out of a jam, ask if there was a way he could have avoided the problem. Is he homeless because he drank and drugged his way out of the community residential rehabilitation center or because there is no low-cost housing available? Move heaven and earth to help the consumer who is working on recovery but cannot find a place to live.

Celestial relocation may not be appropriate for the person who was given the option of appropriate housing but chose not to follow the rules. Confronting in this instance would be to require him to attend AA or NA meetings every day while paperwork is processed for another housing facility. Enabling would be to arrange another bed for him without stipulating that he attend treatment or prove he is serious about treatment.

CASE ILLUSTRATION 7: DIFFICULT CHOICES
David reported being robbed of his Supplemental Security Income check two months in a row. When asked about the

robberies he said they occurred when he was visiting friends in a neighborhood known for drug sales. Both times David's treatment team intervened to ensure that he had food and rent money. It was argued that not having food and rent money would be so stressful that he would end up in a psychiatric hospital. However, when David reported a third robbery, his treatment team disagreed about what should be done. Several members argued that while it was unlikely that he had been robbed three times in a row, it was possible. David had significant psychiatric symptoms and was not known for having good judgment. Without assistance he was likely to become homeless. Other members of the team argued that providing further assistance constituted enabling. Why would David not spend his money on drugs when he knows the treatment team will provide for his needs and bail him out of trouble?

No one felt comfortable with the idea of David living in a homeless shelter. On the other hand, he had been given the option of supervised housing and long-term residential rehabilitation in the past. He had refused the housing when he was told regular drug screens and attendance at Twelve Step meetings were required by these residential programs. In the end, the treatment team agreed that David had been provided with options and had chosen the course of action that led to his homelessness. They did not intervene on his behalf with his landlord, and he was given thirty days to vacate his apartment.

David never went to the shelter; his sister took him in. He eventually agreed to go to a drug and alcohol rehabilitation center. A home visit the week after the "robbery" revealed that he had enough money left to buy nine cases of beer.

The Point Is . . .

1. Some consumers will choose to use alcohol and other drugs, relying on the treatment team to meet their needs.
2. The treatment team should provide options. The consumer decides whether to take those options. The team may not want to shield a consumer from the negative consequences of choosing not to take an appropriate option.

Doing it yourself

Some professionals confuse their attitudes about alcohol and other drugs, their own use, and their perceived abilities with real reasons not to provide treatment. In this respect, they may be delusional. Because of their own use of alcohol and other drugs, some clinicians are uncomfortable even confronting substance abuse.

"I'm hitting happy hour after work. How am I supposed to tell Joellen not to drink?" This clinician is missing the point. The consumer is likely to have more problems with substance use. Joellen may have something wrong with her central nervous system. Certain chemicals within her brain may be out of balance. Ingesting other chemicals that further alter the balance is not a good idea. Illegal chemicals may have an unpredictable effect on her. It is not uncommon for a consumer to have idiosyncratic reactions to alcohol and other drugs. These substances cloud the diagnostic picture, reducing the chances that she will get the proper treatment.

The consumer may have a built-in reason to use alcohol and other drugs. Having a mental illness may leave her chronically anxious and depressed. She may always have the need to "take the edge off." Once she starts using chemicals, she may find it very difficult to stop. Because chemicals work well in the short term, she may resist participating in treatment. She will learn that many street drugs work instantly while some psychotropic medications take weeks. The long term may seem irrelevant to her. Therefore, long-term solutions may seem irrelevant as well.

Once she starts using alcohol and other drugs, her reasons to continue may feed on themselves. If she uses certain substances to ease her psychiatric symptoms, the withdrawal may create more symptoms, which she may try to treat with more of that substance. She may become anxious and depressed. Hallucinations that were once background noise become a steady stream of shouted insults that seem bearable only when she is high. No boss has ever ridden a staff member the way persecutory voices can ride someone with schizophrenia. Imagine a team of invisible but psychotic drill instructors who can read your mind. They join you in your morning shower and scream at you all day long and well into the night. Using alcohol and other drugs provides momentary peace; but when the chemical wears off, the voices come back with a vengeance. For the consumer, the consequences of picking up the first drink or drug can be very harsh.

Finally, the consumer may be on medications that do not mix well with alcohol and other drugs. Some substances lessen the effectiveness of psychotropic medications. Because of this, many consumers are on higher doses of medication than they would need if they abstained from substances. The more medication someone is prescribed, the less likely she is to take all of it. She may even decide not to take any of it.

―――――――――

Food for Thought

The staff member not on psychotropic medications may not appreciate a consumer's desire to take as little medication as possible. Look in your medicine cabinet. If you have several half-empty bottles of medications that were supposed to be taken "until gone," you have some idea why consumers do not always take their medications as prescribed. Imagine that the antibiotic you never finished was a stigmatized medication. Might you have quit taking it even sooner than you did? Perhaps as soon as you felt even slightly better?

―――――――――

Using alcohol and other drugs may create symptoms that are then treated with more psychotropic medications. The treatment team may not be aware that the symptoms are the result of substance abuse. Side effects may intensify because of a combination of substance abuse and subsequent larger doses of psychotropic medication. Once the consumer has had a bad reaction to a medication, she may refuse to take even a small dose of that or any other medication. Someone who got food poisoning from a particular dish and refused to ever eat that dish again has some idea how the consumer feels. "Sure, you say it's going to be different this time, but I'm not going through *that* again," the consumer says. "My whole body went stiff as a board. My toes curled under. I'd rather face a hangover than that any day."

The consequences for substance abuse may be more severe for consumers. Very few staff members end up in seclusion on a psychiatric inpatient unit after a binge. Very few consumers can afford an attorney to get them community service rather than thirty days in jail.

Poor me, poor me, pour me another

Pity is the dagger that enabling uses to kill potential. Buried deep in the most impaired of consumers is the spark of hidden potential. The first time you say, "He might as well drink," you may kill that potential. Part of the reason he looks so bad is that he is staggering under the weight of two or more illnesses. Consumers who come to grips with their illnesses make the most amazing recoveries. If you pity consumers because of their current appearance, they may never reach their potential. Pity kills.

The Point Is . . .

A strange arithmetic governs the interplay of mental illness and substance abuse. The two illnesses together create much more damage than either alone. Curing one illness at a time would eliminate 75 percent of the problem, but neither illness can be cured separately. Neither illness can be cured completely. That is why treatment must be ongoing, at the same time, in the same place, using the same people.

Knowing enough

Too many professionals do not want to treat both mental illness and substance abuse because they do not think they are competent to do so. Initially treating both is more a question of common sense than technique. Not treating them is like letting someone starve to death because you are not a gourmet chef. Mastering a few recipes can make all the difference. Learn the basics and help consumers now. Expand your knowledge of substance abuse and mental illness and be even more effective later.

A good first step is to go to Twelve Step meetings (most meetings are open to the public) to learn about recovery from substance abuse. That is where the experts are. Listen quietly and you will hear how an essentially leaderless group of sufferers overcame a debilitating illness. You will learn how people steadfastly refused to let their potential be buried.

Attending enough meetings will provide a growing awareness of how Twelve Step programs work, not just the mechanics, but the whole program. One can be cheered by hearing about the recovery of people who carried a variety of psychiatric diagnoses and quit using alcohol and other drugs.

Murphy's Other Laws of Psychotropics

1. Someone with two weeks of clean time will hold more sway than the psychiatrist who has worked with the consumer for ten years.

2. If ninety-nine out of a hundred people at an Alcoholics Anonymous meeting see nothing wrong with taking psychotropics (as prescribed by a doctor knowledgeable about addiction), the consumer will find and hang on every word of that hundredth member who believes no one in Alcoholics Anonymous should ever use psychotropic medication.

———•◦•———

The professional who knows how Twelve Step programs work can provide two vital services. First, you can help people use Twelve Step programs in the community. Second, you can set up programs that are adapted to your population. It is that simple. Act as an access ramp to AA and NA. Provide an alternative geared to mentally ill, substance abusing consumers. There is no reason to ignore chemical abuse or to act incompetently. It helps to know about mental illness and substance abuse, but not being an expert in both fields is no excuse for not helping someone.

Using and adapting Twelve Step programs is discussed in chapter 11. Alternatives to AA and NA, such as Rational Recovery, have not been mentioned here because at present their meetings are too few. If you find an alternative to Twelve Step programs, learn about their methods and apply what is useful. (As they say in Alcoholics Anonymous, "Take what you need and leave the rest.") It may help to imagine you are a consumer as you attend alternative programs. How comfortable would a consumer feel at an alternative meeting? How would she receive their message?

There are numerous training materials on treating mental illness. Learn as much as possible. It is not easy to overcome mental illness and substance abuse. While learning about mental illness, try to imagine how appealing alcohol and other drugs might be to someone with a particular disorder.

———•·•———

Warning

Never pretend to know more than you do, but don't assume you do not know enough. Spending one minute in a crack house is not necessary to help a consumer. Knowing all the names for street drugs is not essential. Nor is experiencing hallucinations necessary to help people cope with schizophrenia. Similarly, being in recovery is not a requirement for working with people who abuse substances. Being burned in the fire is not a prerequisite to helping someone rebuild her house. You only have to know how. The professional who is learning about Twelve Step programs and mental illness can help the consumer rebuild her life.

———•·•———

Wearing out

Clinicians can become frustrated with a consumer. They can see clearly that substance abuse harms him. His family is heartbroken over his steady decline. All parties involved remember a time when he was free of substance abuse and mental illness. Many times someone has said, "If we could just get him off those drugs, maybe we could help him." He has no interest in treatment.

There is a tendency for clinicians to write off such difficult consumers and work with only the most "motivated" ones. "He's not going to recover so let's give him the medications (or withhold the medications, or hospitalize him, and so on) and wait for him to decide he wants help." The clinicians may believe that he has got to want help to benefit from it. Those around the consumer begin to, or continue to, enable out of their own frustration. This is a big mistake.

Marinda recently celebrated twelve years of continuous sobriety. For eight years she went to AA meetings and secretly drank screwdrivers from a thermos. If you were her clinician, by year seven would you have been tempted to give up? Knowing that she had been diagnosed with schizophrenia, might it have been tempting to say, "She is just too impaired to understand the Twelve Step program"?

It can take years for some consumers to settle into recovery. Measuring success by how many people are abstaining from chemicals may be very depressing. It may be better to consider how many meetings people attended. How many times have you tried to educate consumers about substance abuse, addiction, and mental illness? What programs are offered at your clinic? Assess your efforts and consistency rather than their recovery. Do not enable a consumer because he has not gotten clean in what you think is an appropriate amount of time. Keep trying. Lead that horse to water often enough and he will be so thirsty from the trip that he will drink. Consumers may eventually become "thirsty for recovery" from your repeated efforts to help.

It is important to keep confronting a consumer about his substance abuse even if you do not think it is having an effect. Too often professionals throw in the towel if the consumer continues to use alcohol and other drugs. He may be on the verge of recovery from substance abuse. It is very common for a consumer to use alcohol and other drugs most heavily just prior to quitting completely and buying into recovery. Often substance use escalates into a crisis that opens the consumer's eyes to the damage he is doing to himself. It is during that crisis that he may remember what you have been saying for weeks, months, or years: "Abstain from alcohol and other drugs, comply with treatment, and your life will improve." It would be tragic if just prior to the eye-opening tragedy the last thing he heard was, "You're hopeless! Forget about medications, therapy, and the Twelve Steps—I'm going to get a new job." A positive attitude *before* a crisis can make a difference.

Seeing things differently

Keep in mind that both mental illness and substance abuse are biopsychosocial illnesses—that is, they have biological, psychological, and social components.

First, consider the *biological* component. Both mental illness and a tendency to develop a substance abuse disorder are likely to be inherited. This does not mean that mentally ill or substance-abusing parents *always* have mentally ill or substance-abusing children. However, the children of mentally ill and/or substance-abusing parents are more likely to develop a mental illness or abuse alcohol and other drugs under certain circumstances. Still, it is not anybody's fault that the consumer developed a mental illness or substance abuse disorder.

Both persistent mental illness and substance abuse can be chronic problems that may last a lifetime. They are "in the bones" so to speak, part of the consumer's physiological being. On the other hand, they are very treatable and can go into long remissions.

While the consumer is not responsible for being predisposed to mental illness and substance abuse, she must take responsibility for participating in appropriate treatment and complying with a recovery plan. The catch is that sometimes consumers do not realize they have either illness and are therefore reluctant to accept treatment. Help them see that they need help. Hold the consumer responsible for getting treatment without blaming her for having either illness.

Try to remind consumers of the positive. Both mental illness and substance abuse can stay in remission for years. New medications are being introduced that are very effective in treating a number of psychiatric symptoms. In addition, new treatment programs are springing up that help people recover from substance abuse and mental illness. The outlook for people coping with both illnesses is definitely improving.

Psychologically, both mental illness and substance abuse can have a strong impact on the way people think. They alter the information coming into the brain by changing the way things outside the body are perceived. Similarly, distortions in thinking can cause or worsen symptoms such as anxiety or depression.

Someone who abuses alcohol and other drugs and has a mental illness may have difficulty trying to concentrate or remember. The tone of someone's voice can suddenly seem much more threatening than it did when the consumer was not under the influence of alcohol and other drugs. Paranoia and fear may result from looking at the world differently while abusing substances. It may occur to the consumer who smokes crack that the police are driving by her building much more than usual. Has someone turned her in? One of her neighbors maybe? Are they watching her now? Perhaps even signaling the police from a nearby window? She feels threatened and angry. At some point she may decide that if she does not "get" them, they will "get" her.

Mental illnesses can have effects very similar to substance abuse. They affect the way people see the world. In extreme cases a consumer may hear voices or see things that are not there. She may suffer from delusions, such as thinking people are plotting against her. She may become anxious or depressed or both. The phobic consumer may perceive tunnels and elevators as dangerous places to be avoided at all costs. Her fears may imprison her in her own home.

Drug and alcohol abuse may change a consumer's behavior. She may become more guarded and reclusive. Before she started abusing crack, she was outgoing and personable. After she starts using alcohol and other drugs, she may begin to avoid people. Her relationships may change. As she changes, the *social* aspects of her life change. People may start to avoid her. They may start to assume more responsibility for her, doing things she used to do for herself. Her whole family may be caught up in covering up her substance abuse or shielding her from the consequences of her behaviors. Her use can have a profound and lasting effect on everyone around her.

Mental illness can also influence a consumer's behavior and the way people interact with her. Some consumers become reclusive and withdrawn. Others behave in outlandish ways, sometimes placing themselves in danger. Many act in ways that embarrass their family members. The people around the consumer often change their own behavior to deal with her illness. As with the substance-abusing consumer, family members may withdraw. Other family members may become caretakers, performing tasks she once did. Worse, they may do things for her that she is still able to do for herself.

Try to see the consumer as having two illnesses with biological predispositions, psychological manifestations, and large social consequences. Seeing the consumer as a weak-willed, amoral, drug abuser who punishes everyone around her makes it more difficult to provide quality care.

CHAPTER 5

COPING WITH SYMPTOMS: A CONSUMER'S EYE VIEW

This chapter highlights the importance of seeing the consumer's point of view. To avoid frustration with the uncertain pace of a consumer's recovery, you need to see what obstacles lie in his path. It is just as important to examine his attitudes as your own.

The paradox

As a treatment professional, you must do everything possible to understand what it feels like to be the consumer. Yet you must never allow the consumer to use her situation as a reason for substance abuse. The professional must encourage, and hopefully admire, the consumer for her efforts to abstain from alcohol and other drugs and to participate in treating her mental illness. You should also understand the pressures on the consumer to use alcohol and other drugs, not taking it personally when she does. Yet professionals must consistently stress abstinence and a negotiated compliance with treatment, no matter how overwhelming life becomes for the consumer.

To better understand the consumer's struggle, put yourself in her shoes. Doing so allows you to cheer her efforts without personalizing her "resistance" or relapses. Her struggles may amaze and inspire you.

Anyone who remains sober despite anxiety, depression, mood swings, phobias, despair, sleeplessness, public apathy and antipathy, persecutory hallucinations, paranoia, side effects from psychotropic medications, flashbacks, and horrendous living conditions is no less inspiring than the physically challenged person who learns to walk again. How many people could stay sober if all day long they heard a voice outside their heads saying, "Sooner or later you're going to relapse"? (That might be the kindest thing a voice might say to someone.)

Imagine being severely agoraphobic and trying to stop abusing benzodiazepines such as Valium or Ativan. On the verge of a panic attack, your arms and legs tremble. You start questioning your decision not to take a drug like Ativan. Sweaty palms and a racing heart warn that soon it will be difficult to catch your breath. Your head fills with fears that most people would brush off but which scare you. Knowing that other people scoff at these fears increases your sense of isolation. The death-cold numbness of a bottle stares out at you as you walk past the liquor store on your way to a Twelve Step meeting. You think, *It was the pills that got me into trouble. Would one drink really hurt me?*

Somehow you go to the meeting, not picking up the first drink. Slowly, painfully, the arduous process of recovery from substance abuse begins. Having taken the first tentative step towards mastering panic, you are truly someone to be admired.

Small is a relative term

Cheating yourself of the small victories can contribute to burnout. If someone stays at an NA meeting for *only* ten minutes, do not write it off as a failure. It is not so much what was accomplished but what the consumer had to go through to do it. The agoraphobic consumer who stayed at an NA meeting for ten minutes may have proven to himself that he can get out of the house, past the liquor store five blocks from his home to a meeting room full of people. Rather than admire him for making such an effort, you may feel disappointed that he did not stay. Do this often enough and you will begin to wonder if you are making a difference.

Food for Thought

Our society uses a bizarre yardstick in deciding whose struggles are publicly admirable and whose are to be carried out in private. The brain sits atop the spinal cord which is connected to the nerves. The higher up the spinal cord that someone is injured, the more amazed we are by his adaptation. And rightly so. The more impaired a person is, the more strength and perseverance it takes to rally his capabilities. Why then, does this appreciation for the struggle seem to evaporate when the problem is at the top of the central nervous system (CNS), the brain? Are people with mental illnesses any less heroic than people with physical challenges when both overcome great obstacles to succeed? The only difference is that mental disabilities cannot be seen and are, therefore, often discounted by the general public. People make a circling motion around their temple to signal insanity. Would they grab their legs to taunt someone in a wheelchair? Some of the bravest people alive are recovering from damage to their CNS. It is most unfortunate that the struggle is so little understood.

In tough economic times the rates of substance abuse, mental illness, and violence skyrocket. As treatment professionals, we do not take this personally. If someone loses his job, becomes depressed, and starts to drink, the professional's ability to help is not questioned. Accepting two ideas will make it easier to deal with this consumer. First, given the person's circumstances, it is not surprising that he is depressed and abusing substances. Second, substance abuse is not going to solve the problem. In fact, the AA and NA slogan *There is no problem so bad a drink or drug won't make it worse* is emphasized.

Too often members of the treatment team take it personally when consumers relapse. Some forget that what is going on inside people can be just as miserable as what is going on around them. They get angry that the consumer is not getting over his illnesses fast enough (to suit the treatment team). They fail to recognize that even though he is not wearing a cast or a bandage, the consumer is in pain. He may still believe that alcohol and other drugs will cure his suffering. Or he may believe that someone suffering as he is has no hope of recovery. If he is not abstaining and compliant, it does not mean he is not in pain and that he does not want to get better.

Some treatment professionals recognize the consumer's pain but use it as justification for his abuse of alcohol and other drugs. They argue that if they were that miserable, they would abuse substances too. Remember the paradox: recognize how painful consumers' lives can be, but *never* use that recognition to justify substance abuse.

CASE ILLUSTRATION 8: WHEN ONE IS WAY TOO MANY
Joel describes his life as consisting of two unintelligible worlds. His inner world is filled with racing thoughts and garbled messages—he is never quite sure what he has seen or heard. He is unable to predict how he is going to respond to anything from the outer world that bumps into his inner world. He finds himself laughing at funerals because he is not sure how he feels about death or if he understands what the minister is saying or if he is dead. He has no firm, consistent mental footing.

Somewhere between his inner world and his outer world lie what we call "hallucinations" and what he calls "them." Sometimes he sees them as we do, a misfunction of some auditory circuit. Other days he sees them as an entity in and of themselves. He argues that they occupy a location. He can point to them even though he cannot see them. Sometimes they sound as if they are speaking from just behind his ear; sometimes they are right over his head; sometimes they sound as if they are standing right in front of him. Besides location they have knowledge. They know what he is thinking and have access to all his memories. They are also clairvoyant, accurately predicting what he is going to do or say. They know people are staring at him before he does. They will say, "She's staring because she thinks you're strange," and when he turns to look she is turning away.

What is most frightening is that the voices have power. They have told him in no uncertain terms that he will face dire consequences if he ignores them. On a bad day they know, predict, and threaten. They hold great sway over how he interprets the outer world, constantly commenting and criticizing.

The outer world is the least understandable realm of his experience. As he goes through the day, he is haunted by nagging doubts about other people's motives. Many of their actions seem to suggest some kind of united effort to harm him in some vague way. He was appalled when his residential counselor suggested that he get his psychotropic medications by injection. They said on TV that using needles spreads AIDS! They gave him an injection in the hospital that put him "to sleep," but he woke up with his arms and legs strapped to the bed. He cannot understand why mental health professionals are so eager for him to take meds. "You were wrong to trust this guy," the voice told him after it was suggested he get an injection. "Better to trust us in the future," another voice added.

People tend to shy away from Joel. Strangers rarely make eye contact. When he tries to strike up a conversation, they become fidgety and often leave on some pretext. He is in a chronic state of "not getting it," that sense that everyone else is privy to some joke that he does not understand. Worse is the accompanying sense that they are laughing all the harder because he does not understand. All the while the voices hammer away at him, "Look what the idiot is doing now."

This man has lost most of his dreams. He is often confused and is persecuted by voices that he is not sure do not exist. He is somewhat paranoid or justifiably fearful depending on your point of view. And he is isolated. His life hurts.

The Point Is . . .

1. Many people with mental illness turn to alcohol and other drugs to deal with symptoms.
2. Substance abuse is likely to make the symptoms of mental illness unmanageable.
3. Consumers may then use more alcohol and other drugs to try to deal with symptoms that have gotten worse because of substance abuse.

Living in the chemical culture

Our culture is awash in chemicals and chemical fantasies. In "beerland" all the men have washboard stomachs that dazzle women wearing tiny bikinis. Drink the right beer and these women will don blond wigs and drop from the sky to serve you lobster by streams laden with gold nuggets. Billboards advertising liquor proclaim "TGI5" (presumably "thank God it's five o'clock"). Women swoon at the sight of a man bold enough to drink certain malt liquors. There is no stigma in these commercials. People interact freely and everyone seems to be having a good time. Magical things seem commonplace and everyone is someone. Life in these commercials contrasts starkly with the way many consumers live. These commercials promise far more than most social service agencies provide. They may make a socially encouraged chemical like alcohol seem very attractive.

Alcohol is in a class by itself because it is not only tolerated but also encouraged. And not just through advertising, but by society as a whole. Alcohol is used to ease social tensions and help people bond. Often someone abstaining from alcohol is encouraged to have "just one" or to "join the party." For someone who already feels alienated this can be powerfully persuasive, especially if anxiety is a pervasive symptom of her mental illness.

Alcohol is also accepted as a self-prescribed antianxiety drug. It is common to hear people talking about "having one to take the edge off." TGIF implies that if we can all just hang in there until five o'clock, there is a shot of whiskey waiting at the end of that stress-ridden rainbow.

The problem is, what about people who feel stressed most of the time? Would they not want to "take the edge off" all of the time? Too often consumers develop a number of physical difficulties because of stress and anxiety. Not the least of these is dependency on alcohol and other drugs.

For example, a group of consumers was discussing a beer commercial that caught their fancy. One person remarked on a series of commercials where people involved in stressful situations turned to the camera and in a deadpan manner said, "Boy, could I go for a _____ now," naming a certain beer. Group members wanted to make their own commercial where they would look at the camera and say, "I was on my way to college on a full scholarship when I got sick. Now I live in a roach-infested apartment in a bad part of town. The voices won't leave me alone and I think the CIA has tapped my phone. Boy, could I go for a _____ now!"

Other drugs seem equally attractive to consumers. For the depressed consumer who still has the energy to chase drugs, the warnings of mental health and chemical dependency counselors may fall on deaf ears. As treatment professionals, we say, "If you smoke crack, you will be more depressed later." She cannot imagine feeling any worse. She knows Prozac is going to take at least three weeks to work, probably longer because she has been drinking and not telling you about it. So when the dealer comes to the door on check day, fifteen minutes of euphoria may seem like heaven. Maybe Prozac will cushion the fall, she reasons. How much worse can it get? She is a good candidate for drug abuse not because of anything the treatment team has or has not done, but because of who and where she is.

Knowing the consumer is a prime candidate for substance abuse and that an already painful life may get worse, the treatment professional wonders what to do about it. *Be consistent.* Under no circumstances should you endorse substance use. Help the consumer improve her life and celebrate each small victory. Most important, understand her reluctance to participate in treatment without personalizing this resistance. And accept that even when you are consistent about abstinence and compliance, people will choose not to get treatment for a number of reasons.

Developmental delay

Sadly, while many of us were discovering independence, others were coming to grips with mental illness. Many people coping with a significant mental illness do not have access to a car. Some are able to use public transportation, but many depend on family and friends for rides. Many do not own homes. They may not be married or hold jobs. Often they have not acquired many of the trappings of adulthood.

They participate in a system that they may see as infantilizing. Picture yourself being forty-five years old and living with your parents. You are told by a twenty-five-year-old caseworker that she will not process entitlement program documents until you agree to take psychotropic medications. "This document has to be completed by your treatment provider," she says. "You are not in treatment when you are off your meds. Take your meds and we will fill out this form for you."

"You mean I gotta take my meds so you'll help me get back some of the money I put into the system before I got sick?" you ask. *Like a good boy?* you say to yourself.

Drug use may be the one thing the consumer *perceives* as adult that he can do. People who have all the rewards of adulthood still hold on for dear life to their right to use chemicals. It is as if not being able to use alcohol and other drugs will make them less of a man or woman. Is it surprising that someone who has lost so much to mental illness would hold on even more tightly to substance use?

What will people think?

Letting go of alcohol and other drugs is to assume the powerful stigma of an *addict*. Although celebrity confessions of substance abuse have given recovery a fleeting chic image, the inability to control substance use still carries negative judgments. Society views addicts as weak-willed, immoral, untrustworthy, and undesirable individuals. Asking consumers to accept the label *addict* is asking them to accept the harsh judgments that go with it.

Twelve Step groups are anonymous for this very reason. Anonymity helps members avoid the stigma associated with substance abuse.

Anonymity's first cousin is confidentiality. And unlike anonymity, confidentiality is legally enforceable. Hospitals that do not protect patients' confidentiality find themselves in court wishing they had. It is in large part the stigma associated with mental illness that makes us so rabid about confidentiality. Consumers are well aware of both stigmas. Is it so surprising that they are reluctant to accept either one?

Many consumers will choose one or the other for a variety of reasons. Some consumers will decide that they are mentally ill. To the substance abuser it makes sense to be mentally ill. She has some feelings she does not like; she puts something in her body to make the feelings go away. For the consumer who is seeking the "right" drug, the mental health system may appear to be the answer.

Other consumers will decide that they have an addiction. Substance abuse can mimic many of the symptoms of mental illness. Addiction can be a more attractive explanation than mental illness for unusual or uncomfortable feelings, thoughts, or events. For the abuser, abstinence from alcohol and other drugs will usually resolve many problems (Daley 1988). For someone coping with mental illness there are no guarantees. A consumer may think it is better to have problems because of something she has *done*—ingested alcohol and other drugs—rather than something she is—depressed, bipolar, or schizophrenic. (It could be argued that "addict" is something one is, rather than *does*, but that debate may not matter to the consumer.)

It gives some consumers a sense of control to blame their problems on substance abuse. A consumer may say she can quit using substances if things get bad enough. She may not believe she can control a mental illness. She can receive treatment for depression, but it is difficult to just stop being depressed.

Sometimes using alcohol and other drugs is a cover for psychiatric symptoms. Many consumers want friends and family to think symptoms are due to substance abuse: "She just had a little too much to drink." Subconsciously, a consumer may use substance abuse to fool herself. It may be comforting to think problems result from substance abuse rather than mental illness. She may forget which came first but hold on to the notion that all problems began with the onset of substance use and, therefore, all problems will cease with abstinence: "The problems started when I started using and they will stop when I stop using."

If the consumer goes to Twelve Step meetings, she may meet someone who has had similar symptoms that disappeared when he quit using alcohol and other drugs. She may see no need for medications. Unfortunately, sometimes other recovering group members encourage consumers to quit taking medications, though this is far less common than it used to be. The argument seems to be "If I was misdiagnosed and put on medications wrongly, you probably were too." Pressure is sometimes applied by telling the consumer that she is not really clean while she is on "nerve" medications. It is implied that she will never get strong while she is on medications.

This can be music to the ears of the consumer eager to believe she is not mentally ill.

It is a mistake to assume those ears hear your intended message. Most people filter what they hear through experiences, fears, hopes, and expectations. People coping with mental illness may filter what they hear through what others perceive to be delusions.

CASE ILLUSTRATION 9: SEEING THE CONSUMER'S POINT OF VIEW
Ed lives alone in a small apartment in a dangerous neighborhood. He is a poor man with no friends. Adolescents taunt him, and most adults avoid him. Unable to work due to overwhelming fears that co-workers mean to harm him, he lives on a small disability allotment. He spends much of his time drinking beer in front of the TV.

One day he hears a voice outside his head telling him he was meant for better things. He is told to watch for a signal that will be coming. After a thorough search of the house, he concludes that the voice is "not of this world." Remembering biblical teachings from his childhood, he suspects the voice is heavenly in origin.

He knows that a heavenly voice is nothing to scoff at so he starts reading the Bible and watching religious programs to try to make sense of his experience. He discovers that God often talks to man and is especially concerned for the downtrodden. He also discovers that God does not always select the holy or the powerful. Little by little, he begins to feel special, to feel uniquely blessed. He is no longer depressed by his circumstances.

Several months later he is picked up by the police for preaching in traffic. He is taken to a local mental hospital where a resident tells him the voices are not God but auditory hallucinations. The resident prescribes Haldol and sends him home with a follow-up appointment at the community mental health clinic. He is completely unsettled by this experience but refuses to believe the voices are not God.

Ed's first appointment is with an outpatient therapist who happens to have a strong religious background. She asks him to take the Haldol even if he does believe it is God speaking to him. He sees the cross on her desk and agrees.

A month later the voices have stopped. He looks around and becomes despondent. The therapist tries to explain to Ed that his voices are now "under control." She seems very pleased.

"There is no telling how far you can go!" she says. His thinking is still very concrete, and he has no idea where she might want him to "go." He is further confused and depressed by the resident's and therapist's conviction that he is somehow better on this medication. He hates his life and he has dry mouth. He is thoroughly disgusted with the mental health system.

Turning back to the Bible, he discovers that God punishes those who turn their backs on Him. Ed wonders what it feels like to be turned into a pillar of salt. "I'll know soon enough," he says to himself. "Dry mouth may be the first step." He quits taking psychotropic medications and sure enough God speaks to him again.

The Point Is . . .

1. If you put yourself in the consumer's shoes, his actions make perfect sense. If he accepts that God speaks to him, the drabness and disappointments in his life no longer matter. He is unique and "chosen." To accept the mental health system's interpretation of his experience is to accept a drab reality and a treatable, but not curable, illness that is highly stigmatized.

2. To be successful, any intervention with this man must recognize his world view and provide an attractive alternative that fits the data. If he cannot have a special relationship with God, what good is a "cure"?

3. Do not paddle away. The ethical and most helpful intervention is to find a way for him to have God in his life and keep his substance abuse and mental illness in remission. A good starting point might be consulting with the local pastoral counseling center. You may want to help him understand the Twelve Step concepts of a "higher power" and "God as you understand Him."

PART II

TREATMENT STRATEGIES

CHAPTER 6

———·❦·———

FUNDAMENTALS OF DUAL DISORDERS TREATMENT

Clinical interventions are based on a particular philosophy of treatment and recovery. This chapter discusses fundamentals of dual disorders treatment that can help you develop a philosophy of treatment.

Relationships between dual disorders

There are several possible relationships between psychiatric and substance use disorders (Daley, Moss, and Campbell 1993, 6–8; Meyer 1986, 3–16). Psychiatric illness raises the odds of developing a substance use disorder, and a substance disorder raises the odds of developing a psychiatric illness. Consumers with chronic mental illnesses are more vulnerable than others to the adverse effects of alcohol and drugs, even in small quantities. On the other hand, substance use can contribute to the first episode of an underlying psychiatric condition. Or it can play a major role in a recurrence of psychiatric illness after a period of remission.

Psychiatric disorders can modify the course of substance use disorders in several ways. First, consumers with certain types of psychiatric disorders, such as antisocial personality disorder or depression, experience an earlier onset of substance abuse. Second, consumers with borderline or antisocial personality disorders often drop out of treatment prematurely. Third, consumers with a lot of psychiatric symptoms do worse in recovery than those without a lot of psychiatric symptoms. Alternatively, chronic use of alcohol or drugs, acute or long-term withdrawal from alcohol or drugs, and the consequences of substance use can contribute to psychiatric symptoms such as anxiety, depression, and suicidal tendencies. Although psychiatric and substance use disorders can develop separately and be independent disorders, the illnesses of many consumers become closely linked over the course of time. Thus, attempting to assign a "primary" versus "secondary" disorder has limited benefit.

Assessment

Symptoms and problems can change over time. Therefore, assessment of the consumer's disorders, his functioning in various areas of life, and his response to treatment is best viewed as an ongoing process. The longer a consumer is sober, the more psychiatric symptoms may clear—or they may worsen. When possible, use objective measures such as breathalyzers and urinalysis to see if someone is using substances. Also, get information from other sources, such as family members or other social service professionals, to help assess the consumer's situation over time.

Integrated treatment

A number of different approaches to treating mental illness and substance abuse have been proposed, including the sequential, parallel, and integrated treatment models (Minkoff and Drake 1991). We believe integrated treatment is usually the best approach because it focuses on both psychiatric and substance use recovery issues. Although in a given treatment session more emphasis may be placed on one of the disorders, integrated treatment seeks an overall balance.

Motivation of consumers

There are many methods to motivate consumers to enter and stay in treatment and recovery. Consumers coping with mental illness and substance abuse, particularly inpatients, are at high risk to drop out of treatment prematurely. The time and effort spent stabilizing a consumer in an inpatient program may be lost if she fails to keep up outpatient or partial hospital treatment. Low motivation and poor compliance are best viewed as a problem of treatment systems and counselors rather than "blamed" on consumers. Here are some interventions that may increase consumer involvement in ongoing partial hospital or outpatient treatment:

- Motivational counseling
- Reminders of scheduled treatment sessions in early recovery, such as phone calls or letters
- Reinforcement for attending treatment sessions such as bus tickets, points that accumulate and can be cashed in for vouchers for food or merchandise
- Accessible counselors and staff members (consumers don't have to wait for weeks for appointments)
- Assistance with practical life problems that interfere with attending sessions, such as child care, transportation, housing, and economic problems
- Outreach for consumers who fail to show up for treatment appointments, such as home visits, phone calls, or letters
- Use of casemanagers to access entitlement programs, seek help from outside agencies, and solve day-to-day practical problems

Therapeutic alliance

The therapeutic alliance you build with a consumer is an important variable in treatment compliance and outcome. Although many counselors attribute treatment progress solely to the consumer, everyone involved in a consumer's treatment can affect treatment compliance and outcome. Consumers who develop a therapeutic alliance with staff members are more likely to stay in treatment (Gerstely 1989). Ongoing treatment, in turn, increases the consumer's positive progress. A therapeutic alliance is developed through attentive listening to the consumer, "joining" her where she is in recovery, working together to identify problems and treatment goals, and assuming a nonjudgmental and hopeful attitude about recovery.

Education

Consumer education is important in recovery. Education often paves the way for self-awareness and change. It helps the consumer chip away at denial and provides a cognitive "road map" for recovery. Education can also empower him and raise hope for positive change. Consumers benefit from education on causes, effects, and treatments for their specific disorders. Education on the role of self-help programs is also critical.

Recovery skills

Developing recovery skills is important. Recovery skills can relate to specific disorders. For example, coping with symptoms of an illness, spotting early signs of psychiatric or substance use relapse, and developing structure in daily life are helpful for people with schizophrenia, bipolar disorder, or recurrent depression. Coping with cravings, thoughts of using substances, and pressures from others to use substances are skills needed for recovery from a substance use disorder. Recovery skills can also be "generic," applying to self-improvement regardless of the specific disorders; for example, making amends, improving interpersonal relationships, developing spirituality, becoming assertive, and coping with upsetting feelings are issues common among consumers with various combinations of disorders.

Self-disclosure

Help the consumer talk about his thoughts, feelings, and problems. Self-disclosure is important in developing relationships, solving problems, and overcoming roadblocks in recovery. For example, if a consumer discloses suicidal thoughts or thoughts of using drugs, you can work with him in coping with these issues. However, consumers sometimes tell counselors what they think they want to hear and hesitate to share troubling thoughts, feelings, or personal issues.

Identification of goals

Helping the consumer identify goals provides a focus for treatment. Focusing on solutions and reaching goals empowers the consumer and gives her something to strive towards. When she "owns" the goals, she is much more likely to work toward them than if they are imposed by an "external" source, such as a treatment program.

Medication

Medication is often an important and necessary aspect of recovery. Chronic mental illnesses usually require medication to control acute symptoms and reduce the likelihood of a recurrence of symptoms. Consumers sometimes confuse psychiatric medication with street drugs. Sometimes, peers in support groups encourage consumers to stop taking medication. Attitudes and behaviors about medication need to be talked about, particularly early on when a consumer is likely to stop medication when symptoms worsen or improve.

Support

All efforts of the consumer to recover should be supported, regardless of the outcome. In our culture, we often support and reinforce "outcome" and ignore "efforts" at change. Efforts should be acknowledged, praised, and reinforced even if the results aren't always positive. For example, a consumer who is very negative about AA or NA who finally agrees to attend a meeting should be complimented even if he returns from the meeting with a list of complaints. Or a consumer who finally gets up the nerve to speak his mind and share his anger toward a family member should be complimented for making this effort, even if the family member wasn't receptive to what he had to say.

Community resources

Many consumers need help in using community resources. Consumers with chronic mental disorders often have medical, economic, housing, legal, interpersonal, educational, job, and recreational problems. Helping them deal with sometimes intimidating community agencies, such as public assistance, public housing, or a dual-disorders residential program or school, can be very beneficial. Even seemingly small interventions, such as teaching them how to negotiate smaller payments on a utility bill or fill out an application for government benefits, can be immensely helpful.

Family

Talking to the family or significant others, when appropriate, can help and support the consumer in numerous ways. They are valuable sources of information during the initial assessment and during ongoing recovery (see chapter 13).

Self-help groups

Self-help support groups for addiction, mental health disorders, and dual disorders provide a valuable source of help for consumers. They offer much that professionals can't. Consumers should be educated about support groups, exposed to specific groups, and encouraged to use the "tools" of the various programs (see chapter 11 on Twelve Step programs). If a consumer rejects the notion of support groups, explore her reasoning and continue to encourage the use of groups. Our experience shows that the majority of consumers will eventually attend support groups—some just take longer to see the benefits.

Phases of treatment

Clinicians and researchers have identified phases of recovery for people coping with mental illness and substance abuse (Daley and Thase in press; Kaufman 1989). Each phase has a number of potential therapeutic issues, clinical interventions, and possible outcomes. For example, during the stabilization phase, the common therapeutic issues include acute symptoms of psychiatric illness or substance abuse, denial, cravings for substances, and the need for family and social support. Possible interventions include detoxification, medication, review of the consumer's history of symptoms, craving management, Twelve Step work, and family sessions. Progress is seen when the consumer accepts he has at least two problems, feels hopeful about recovery, becomes drug- and alcohol-free, and stabilizes from acute psychiatric symptoms.

Consumers progress through recovery phases at different rates. Rarely do they move in order from one phase to the next—often, a consumer will move back and forth between phases. However, some consumers don't progress much beyond the first few phases of recovery.

Persistent symptoms

Some persistent symptoms of psychiatric illness may never totally leave or may come and go over time. Consumers and clinicians alike can fall into the trap of expecting all symptoms to stop. For some consumers, this is unrealistic and unlikely. Consumers often have to learn to live with some symptoms, such as chronic anxiety, depression, obsessions, hallucinations, delusions. If suffering is reduced and symptoms don't interfere as much with the consumer's life, she is making progress.

Setbacks

Relapse prevention is an excellent focus of treatment once the consumer is stabilized and has established a foundation for recovery. However, many consumers will have setbacks. Some will have minor periods of substance use, while others will get back into a full-blown addiction. Some will have minor exacerbations of psychiatric symptoms, while others will experience a new episode of illness. Rehospitalization rates are higher for consumers with dual disorders than for those with only one disorder (Green 1988). Consumers can use these setbacks to learn about what went wrong in the past with their recovery and to improve their current efforts at recovery. Setbacks can be used to motivate, teach, or reinforce important aspects of dual disorders and recovery.

CHAPTER 7

Nuts and Bolts Issues
In Daily Recovery

Sometimes just getting through the day can be a challenge for consumers. This chapter addresses some of the common day-to-day problems consumers experience, especially in the early weeks and months of recovery.

Coping with cravings

Cravings can kill recovery. A body used to a certain substance often reacts badly when that substance is taken away. And reminders of the substance pop up everywhere. A newly recovering beer drinker cannot watch an hour of TV without hearing a sales pitch on the virtues of some new beer. As he watches a sporting event, every break in the action is filled with images of new brews that are cold, frozen, dry, or just different.

Since a consumer may complain of experiencing cravings "out of the blue," it helps to *plan in advance* what he will do if he experiences cravings. Part of the plan may include waiting for the cravings to pass, getting busy, considering the consequences of using alcohol and other drugs, eliminating the cause of the craving, calling someone in recovery, going to a Twelve Step meeting, and learning to deal with feelings.

The simplest solution is often to *wait for the cravings to pass.* Cravings usually are short lived. Point out that cravings reach a peak and then subside. Wait long enough and they will go away. Give in to them, and the craving may be even worse the next time.

A consumer may perceive cravings for substances as long lasting. The worst thing he can do is to sit and think about the craving. Advise him to *get busy* when he experiences cravings. Encourage him to do something to take his mind off the craving. One consumer joked that "clean time" really referred to time in his apartment. Whenever he experienced cravings at night, he would clean his apartment. Scrubbing the linoleum in front of his toilet brought back memories that chased away his craving for alcohol and other drugs.

Suggest doing something with another recovering person, if at all possible. Sometimes a consumer may have cravings late at night when no one is available. In this case he may have to find something to do until the craving passes. For example, advise him to try to get to sleep. Even the most addicted person finds it difficult to use alcohol and other drugs in his sleep.

Sometimes a consumer can be very creative in dealing with cravings. A man who associated his cravings with a particular corner of his apartment would stand in front of that corner and curse his cravings. While this may seem odd, it worked for him.

Another consumer woke up missing the first marijuana high of the day and thinking a lot about it. So he decided to walk to help curb his craving and take his mind off it. Each morning he got out of bed, put on sweatpants and a shirt, and went walking until the craving passed. At first, his walks were tortuous. With each step he would tell himself he was not going to "pick up" the first joint. As time went on, his walks got to be more and more enjoyable. The surprise bonus for him was that he began to lose weight.

One of the best strategies the consumer can use is to *call someone* else in recovery who has experienced cravings. The recovering person may have helpful suggestions. Or he may have been through the same situation and can encourage the consumer to "tough it out." Often simply talking about cravings helps to decrease them. Encourage consumers to get phone numbers of others in recovery and to keep a list of telephone numbers for local Twelve Step groups, hotlines, and their treatment facility by their phones or in their wallets.

Going to a Twelve Step meeting often helps. Meetings provide a safe haven from chemicals and a place for consumers to talk about their cravings. They're also a great alternative to bars because they provide a place to socialize and find support.

Teach consumers to *consider the consequences* of using alcohol and other drugs. It helps to compile a list of things that have happened when the consumer was abusing alcohol and other drugs. Help him list the things that might happen if he gave in to the craving. This list can be used to decide whether getting high is worth the potential consequences. This cost-benefit analysis allows the consumer to ask himself, "What do I get out of using alcohol and other drugs? What does it cost me?"

Sometimes a consumer can link cravings to a specific trigger. In the past he may have used alcohol and other drugs to deal with unpleasant feelings and events. When these feelings and events occur, he may find himself craving substances. Teach people to identify anything that might stir up cravings, and teach them strategies to cope without using.

One man used to get high watching late-night movies. When he first quit using alcohol and other drugs, he started going to bed early, not staying up late to watch movies. After several months of abstaining from alcohol and other drugs, he began to stay up later and later. "Out of the blue" his cravings returned. After he realized he was following old patterns, he was able to identify the source of his cravings. He gradually learned to watch movies without strong cravings.

Coping with people, places, and things

Sometimes a consumer will feel pressured to use alcohol and other drugs by people she cannot avoid. If she lives with a substance-abusing parent, she may feel pressured to resume her own consumption of alcohol and other drugs. Try to convince the consumer that she is endangering her newfound sobriety. Point out to her and to the other person that she is very vulnerable to the effects of alcohol and other drugs. The consumer needs a place to be other than around someone who is pressuring her to use. Try to provide a place at your facility or another agency. (Drop-in centers can be an excellent resource if the consumer is drug-free.) Friends and family members may try in a number of ways to persuade the consumer to use substances. No matter what their argument, certain facts cannot be ignored.

It is the consumer who must face the consequences of substance abuse. The consumer's uncle, who tries to convince her to "lighten up and have a beer," has probably never been hospitalized because of the alcohol and other drugs the consumer used.

Medications do not mix with alcohol and other drugs. The uncle urging the consumer to use alcohol and other drugs is probably not taking psychotropic medications. He may have no idea of the dangers of mixing the two. If the person urging the consumer to use alcohol and other drugs is on medications, ask the consumer how stable this person is. Chances are he is not all that stable.

If there is something wrong with the consumer's central nervous system, she may suffer more from the effects of substance abuse than the person urging her to use alcohol and other drugs. What may be harmless to the person without a mental illness may be devastating to the person *with* a mental illness.

Help consumers practice saying no. Have her describe a situation in which she might feel pressured to use alcohol and other drugs. Then "play out" the scene, allowing her to rehearse saying no to substance abuse. It is important that consumers learn refusal skills *before* they feel pressured to use alcohol and other drugs. This may require a lot of practice until they are comfortable saying no.

Structuring free time

A recovering consumer may face a lack of structure. Some consumers' lives have deteriorated to the point where they have no spouse, house, job, money, or hobbies. How are these folks to structure their time? Some of them discover that, like many people who abuse substances, they spent much of their time obtaining, using, or recovering from the effects of alcohol and other drugs. Sudden abstinence and compliance can leave the consumer with too much time on his hands.

The consumer may need to relearn how to use his time constructively. Start with the basics. Is there anything he likes to do? (You will be amazed at how many people cannot think of one thing other than using alcohol and other drugs that they like to do.) Reintroduce the consumer to activities he enjoyed before he developed a mental illness or began using alcohol and other drugs. Help him identify and participate in new activities, preferably ones that are easily learned and do not require great amounts of patience. Do not, for example, teach the newly sober how to build ships in a bottle.

See the consumer as often as possible in his early recovery. It is important that he have something to do other than sit around wishing he could get high. Help him plan each and every day. Be as specific as possible. Help him establish a routine. Addicts with years of recovery talk about being on "autopilot" and using a routine that keeps them moving during tough times. One man with eight years of sobriety lost his father in a car crash. He reported that his body insisted on going to AA meetings when his mind wanted to stay home and drown his sorrows.

A consumer may balk at the idea of structuring his day with activities at the treatment center. If so, use this resistance to steer him to noninstitutional meetings and the recovering community. Encourage him to attend Twelve Step meetings or mental health support meetings in the community. It is a chance for him to meet people who understand his need to abstain from alcohol and other drugs. More important, he may meet people who structure their lives around their recovery. What may truly amaze and impress the consumer is that many of these people have fun without alcohol and other drugs. They are sober, not somber.

Coping with psychiatric symptoms

What if the consumer deals with her cravings; changes people, places, and things; copes with social pressures to use alcohol and other drugs; adds structure to her day; and her psychiatric symptoms still return? She may be none too pleased that she has gone to such effort and still suffers from symptoms of mental illness.

It may help to point out that there is no problem so bad alcohol and other drugs won't make worse. At least without all the alcohol and other drugs in her system the two of you will have a better idea of what is wrong. Without alcohol and other drugs to interfere, there is a better chance that psychotropic medications and counseling will be effective.

Next, establish a plan of action for dealing with specific psychiatric symptoms. What is it the two of you intend to do about her depression? What should she do if the voices come back? How will she get through a panic attack or cope with avoidant behavior? Help her plan a strategy for dealing with symptoms *before* they occur.

Part of the plan should be an agreement about what will be done if she has certain symptoms. If, for example, a consumer has made numerous suicide attempts shortly after dropping out of treatment, negotiate what to do if she misses two appointments in a row or has persistent thoughts about dropping out of treatment. This plan may include, for example, a suicide prevention contract in which she agrees to take specific steps when she feels suicidal.

Coping with remission

Sadly, one of the toughest things for consumers to deal with is complete remission of both illnesses. The consumer who was medicating his pain and hiding from the world may suddenly realize how many years have gone by and what a mess his life is. He may feel ill-equipped to do anything about it.

Recently a consumer celebrated two years of continuous abstinence from crack. While he was excited to have reached this plateau, he was also somewhat disheartened. He saw that he had wasted many years of his life getting high. He looked around and saw that the neighborhood he had grown up in was now a war zone. Many people he loved were addicted, infected, or dead. He knew there was no cure for his mental illness or his addiction, and that he would have to manage both for the rest of his life.

Usually he was very excited about his recovery, but sometimes it seemed easier just to think about settling back into drug abuse. "I'm glad I saved my potential. But some days it's a struggle just to get to a meeting. 'Potential' just seems like a nice thing I won't ever have the energy to use," he said.

He worried that he was becoming depressed. He needed reassurance that what he felt was appropriate to his circumstances and that *not all feelings are part of mental illness.* He had been getting high for so long that he described his feelings as "lurking out there." His feelings seemed alien, and initially he wanted to have the dosage of his psychotropic medications raised as high as possible. It was only with time that he learned to accept certain feelings as part of the human condition.

He also learned that *painful feelings can be useful.* Often depression, sadness, and pain spur people into making changes in their lives. If they are smart, they make changes that are incompatible with a substance-abusing lifestyle.

Talking about feelings helps the consumer make sense of his experiences. Because feelings can seem so alien to a consumer, he may not be quite sure what he is feeling. More often, he may not be sure if his feelings are appropriate. It may help if you normalize or validate his feelings by pointing out that many people would feel as he does given his circumstances. If appropriate, share your own experiences.

A consumer who had cancer was told that with treatment her chance for survival was fifty-fifty at best. She opted not to be treated and died. One of her friends became very quiet and withdrawn. He quit speaking in group. As time passed and he maintained his reserve, his clinician became concerned that the consumer was getting very depressed. After much prodding, the consumer revealed that he was not depressed. He was not sure *what* he felt. With the help of his clinician, he began to see that he was angry and simply ashamed to admit his anger.

This consumer harbored a deep resentment toward his deceased friend. His clinician was able to normalize this by pointing out that for a time, she, too, was very angry with the deceased woman. They agreed that they both missed her and perhaps that was part of their anger. Together they were able to normalize their feelings by talking about them.

Being real

It is important to show that emotions are normal. If a consumer misses twelve straight appointments and then calls your boss to say you are never available, a little anger may be warranted. Pretending never to have any emotions eliminates you as somebody who can normalize the consumer's feelings. Consider the consumer's state of mind and temper your reaction. It is not appropriate to express anger about something the consumer said in the middle of a psychotic state.

Explain to the consumer that your feelings were not hurt by what she said while in the psychiatric hospital, but now that her thinking has cleared, you expect to have a mutually respectful relationship.

Dealing with relapse

It is common for a consumer to use alcohol and other drugs after he has made a commitment to abstain from them. He may need help to get back on the road to recovery. Start by exploring several questions with the consumer.

What led to relapse? Find out how committed the consumer was to abstaining from alcohol and other drugs. Did he resist alcohol and other drugs as long as he could? Had he ever been sold on the idea of abstinence? What people, places, and things did he associate with using substances this time? Who did he use with and why? Outline the pattern of his substance abuse and list what interferes with his efforts to recover.

With this knowledge in mind, ask the consumer, "What could you have done differently to have avoided this last relapse?" Focus on changing the people, places, and things that led up to the use of alcohol and other drugs. Explore the internal factors that led to substance use. How was the consumer feeling prior to using alcohol and other drugs? What was he thinking? What was he doing or not doing? He may need help in changing his mood, thoughts, and behavior. He may also need reassurance that he can get back into recovery right away.

Teach the consumer that waking up the morning after a relapse is like surviving a car crash. He could have been killed. He might have been hurt. Luckily, his body has already been at work trying to heal itself. It is time for him to put his mind to the project. Outline what happened so that it does not happen again. It is not a time to get cocky because he survived or depressed because he slipped. It is time to get to work!

CASE ILLUSTRATION 10: KEEP TRYING

Kathy was a single mother of an eight-year-old boy. She loved her son dearly. She also loved a variety of drugs. She had carried numerous diagnoses. Intellectually, she could see that alcohol and other drugs were a threat to her mental health and to the welfare of her son. On several occasions she had made halfhearted "pledges" to stop using substances. Most often she did this as a condition of her release from a psychiatric hospital. Kathy was quick to point out that her drug use had, in her opinion, never caused her any harm. She did not believe that her use affected her son either because she never used in front of him. When she was hospitalized, her parents kept the boy with them.

One day her father was working in the garden when he suffered a massive heart attack. Two days later he was dead. Kathy went on a binge that lasted over a week. She woke up in the hospital with little recollection of the previous nine days.

As her thinking began to clear, Kathy was smacked down by reality. Her father had been buried without her ever having said good-bye. Her mother had been too depressed to care for her son. An aunt had taken temporary custody of him and had decided to seek permanent legal custody. The aunt told Kathy, "Drug addicts and mental patients make poor mothers, and I'm sorry but you happen to be both."

In order to be released from the hospital, Kathy had to agree to attend outpatient counseling for mental illness and alcohol and other drug abuse problems. At her first outpatient appointment she convinced her therapist that she should only attend once per month because she needed the time to fight for custody of her son. She also convinced her therapist that she did not need to attend drug and alcohol groups at the clinic.

"With all the trouble the drugs caused me, do you think I'd be stupid enough to pick them up again?" Her therapist thought this made sense and handed her an NA meeting list. Two weeks later Kathy missed a court date because she was drunk. She lost custody of her son.

She was assigned a new therapist. This therapist recognized that losing her son must have been excruciatingly painful, but did not, however, accept Kathy's view that an unjust legal system had "illegally taken away her rights." She did not agree to help Kathy get her son back. What the therapist said to Kathy was that she would help her learn the skills she needed to be a good mother. First and foremost,

Kathy had to learn to stay clean from alcohol and drugs, one day at a time.

Once again Kathy asked for an NA meeting list, saying, "I got myself into this mess, and I am going to get myself out." Her therapist reminded her that she had tried it on her own and had lost her son—was she willing to gamble like that again? After much arguing Kathy agreed to plan out her days. She agreed to attend recovery and Twelve Step groups at the clinic and in the community. She agreed to a schedule that initially left her with very few unstructured moments. As she began sticking to her schedule, she was better able to deal with her cravings. She met people at NA groups who had similar cravings and were able to talk her through them. She reestablished contact with her aunt who allowed her to visit her son but steadfastly refused to give up custody.

One day in group, Kathy began to sob and could not seem to stop. She left in the middle of group, went to her apartment, and cried for hours. When she was done, she called her therapist and said she was going to get drunk. She felt that she had given it her best shot but even without alcohol and other drugs she was still too depressed to face life.

Her therapist pointed out that as long as she was clean, she had a chance of regaining custody. She also had Kathy talk about all that had happened prior to group. After much discussion Kathy realized that she had been thinking about her father for days. Her therapist told Kathy that when her own father had died she had taken a leave of absence because she did not think she would be able to deal with other people's sadness.

Together they made three lists. The first was a list of signals that alerted Kathy that she needed to be in the hospital.

They agreed that Kathy would probably be sad for some time but that if she saw more than three of her "signals," she would call her therapist right away. The second list outlined all the signals that Kathy was going to relapse to alcohol or drug use. Kathy agreed that if she got too many signals, she would contact her therapist or an NA member. The third list was made up of all the bad things that had happened to her when she had a relapse of either illness.

A week later Kathy went on another binge and ended up in a psychiatric hospital.

The Point Is . . .

1. No matter what you do, some consumers will not improve. Alcohol and other drugs are too appealing, mental illness can be devastating, and sometimes life is tragic.
2. You have to be happy with doing the best you can. You never know who is going to make an amazing comeback, overcoming both illnesses to lead a stable and rewarding life.
3. Help consumers plan their day, learn the warning signs of relapse of both illnesses, and deal with their emotions.
4. Don't stop paddling.

Staying safe

Not addressing substance abuse can become a safety issue. The more often someone attends a program under the influence of alcohol and other drugs, the greater the chances she will act out, possibly endangering you or other consumers. Intoxicated consumers can be emotional land mines waiting to go off at the slightest provocation. If not confronted, they may go off on another consumer or an unsuspecting colleague. Even if you fear them "going off" on you, confront consumers who are under the influence. Consider yourself part of the "bomb squad."

Someone thought to be intoxicated should be told in no uncertain terms why she is suspected to be under the influence of substances. If you think she has been using alcohol, perform a breathalyzer test. If it registers any alcohol use, remove her from the building. If she is likely to have medical complications, try to steer her to a hospital emergency room or detoxification center. If the complications are life threatening and she refuses to go, consider involuntary commitment.

Do not try to reason with someone who is likely to be under the influence. It may make her feel that even though she has been using alcohol and other drugs, she is still rational—otherwise why would the professionals still be trying to reason with her? It can be dangerous. Consumers using alcohol and other drugs are usually more impulsive than those who are clean and sober.

If the consumer has been using something other than alcohol, try to get a urine sample. But ask yourself first, "How likely is it that I will end up wearing the sample?" Always err on the side of dryness and safety. The reason for getting the sample is to have concrete evidence of substance abuse, but treatment can still be provided without it. Remember to confront consumers for safety, but safely confront them.

Experiencing withdrawal

Withdrawal from alcohol and other drugs can be very unpleasant, but in most cases it is not life threatening. Each program should have a policy on detoxification. It should not be up to the overnight residential counselor to decide whether a consumer should "sleep it off" or be taken to an emergency room. It is better to have medical staff decide in advance when medical help is needed. If, for example, the consumer had medical complications in the past from substance abuse, then there should be a plan in place to deal with his continued use or withdrawal. The plan may be as simple as saying that he will be taken to the emergency room any time staff suspect he has been abusing alcohol or other drugs. More complicated plans might include hourly observations or consultations with physicians. Whatever the plan is, it should be explained to the consumer and agreed upon in advance.

When in doubt, take the consumer to detoxification. If he does not need to be detoxified, he can be sent home. You may feel somewhat foolish when he is sent home, but that feeling is not half as unpleasant as the sinking feeling that you will experience when the ambulance comes to a screeching halt in front of your building. Always err on the side of being safe. Even if the consumer resents being "dragged" to the emergency room or detoxification center, you have at least shown concern.

CHAPTER 8

———

RECOVERY SLOGANS

Slogans provide a window to Twelve Step programs. Understanding slogans gives the consumer a basic idea of how Twelve Step programs deal with day-to-day issues. As a clinician it is important that you understand the slogans in order to help the consumer apply them to her life. Repeated often enough, they become part of the consumer's automatic thinking. They can become the first thought she has when faced with a difficult situation or the temptation to use substances.

This chapter explains several slogans in depth to illustrate their use in treatment. It is hoped that by this point you have attended several Twelve Step meetings and are already familiar with many of the slogans.

- Don't pick up the first drink or drug
- One day at a time
- There is no problem so bad a drink or drug will not make it worse
- HALT: Don't let yourself get too Hungry, Angry, Lonely, or Tired
- Easy does it
- Live and let live
- Let go and let God
- Sober not somber
- First things first
- Turn it over

When discussing slogans with consumers make certain you both have the same understanding of what a slogan means. For example, one consumer thought *One day at a time* meant "bide your time until you can get even." On the other hand, another consumer showed remarkable insight. She hated taking her medications. The very sight of her pill bottles upset her. So each morning she got out enough pills for that day, put the bottles back in her medicine cabinet, and said to herself, "One day at a time." For her the slogan meant that just for that day she would take her medications. She would worry about the rest of the bottle another day.

Don't pick up the first drink or drug

The most basic of the slogans is *Don't pick up the first drink or drug.* The only guaranteed way not to get into trouble with alcohol and other drugs, the cornerstone of recovery, is not to take that first drink or drug. Some people can successfully taper off their drug of choice, but they are rare. Tapering implies control, and by definition, addicts have lost control of their alcohol and other drug use. Even if someone with a mental illness does not meet the classic definition for addiction, he may be more vulnerable to the effects of substance abuse.

Not picking up the first drink or drug eliminates the futile and frustrating attempts to control substance use. To a consumer, controlled use may mean drinking one beer an hour when he really feels like drinking two six-packs as fast as he can. To him, controlled use may mean smoking marijuana only on weekends when he really wants to light up before he gets out of bed. To him, controlled use may mean confining substance use to certain days and then counting the minutes of each hour of each day until that long anticipated moment arrives when he can use—not that he needs it, having abstained for two days, twenty-three hours, and seven minutes.

Not picking up the first drink or drug eliminates the need to switch from drug to drug, brand to brand, and place to place. How many people eliminate their problem by switching from gin to vodka, cocaine to speed, hash to marijuana, and so on because the "real" problem is a low-quality brand, the wrong bar, or a dishonest dealer: "He gave me some bad stuff—that's the problem"?

Food for Thought

Some clinicians balk at the suggestion of abstinence from alcohol and other drugs. Perhaps they have personal issues with abstinence. If so, they are missing the point: for many consumers, using any substances and avoiding psychiatric symptoms are mutually exclusive. Consumers may have different issues than clinicians (psychotropic medications, more dire consequences, a built-in reason to use alcohol and other drugs, and an existing CNS dysfunction). Some consumers lack the judgment to decide how much is too much. Clinicians should not judge consumers' use of alcohol and other drugs by their own standards or values.

Don't pick up the first drink or drug is the opposite of the "might as wells." Teach people that a "might as well" attitude leads to relapse. It is a mistaken assumption that relapse is just around the corner and nothing can be done about it; it is a way for the consumer to excuse himself from responsibility. Not picking up the first drink or drug guarantees that no damage will be caused by that chemical. It greatly improves the chances for serenity and sobriety by providing a rallying point: "No matter what happens I'm not using!"

A consumer may believe he will lose his sobriety the first time he fights with his spouse or attends a social function where alcohol is served. He may say, "I'm sober now, but what about when the kids start acting up?" He is slipping into the "might as wells." It is your job to help him see that no matter what happens, he has the option of not picking up the first drink or other drug.

Don't pick up the first drink or drug is the simplest part of Twelve Step recovery programs. Consumers have no difficulty understanding this slogan, and nothing could be more concrete. In reviewing why someone relapsed, trace the steps that led up to picking up the first drink or drug. It does not matter how much was used or when the consumer ran into problems. The battle was already lost the first time the consumer tried to control his use of substances.

One day at a time

One day at a time is a slogan rich in meaning. Here are some of them.

The past is not now. Many people in treatment for mental illness and substance abuse have horrific pasts. They have spent time in jails, in hospitals, and on the streets. No matter how well things are going now, they may jump at the shadow of their not-so-distant past. It is as if they do not want to get too happy for fear the past will drag them back. Teach people that being happy today builds a happier past. Enjoy today and they can remember it gladly. (Borrow sorrow from yesterday and pay the interest on it tomorrow.) Live one day at a time!

The future is not now. A consumer may fear the future and see no other choice but to start worrying about it now. Remind her that unlike the past, she has some control over the future. Having learned from past mistakes, she is better equipped to deal with the future. She can face it sober. Chances are that without alcohol and other drugs she will be more stable on medications and less likely to be hospitalized. New psychotropic medications (Zoloft, Clozaril, and Risperdal) offer hope for a less symptomatic life. If she gets involved in treatment, she stands a better chance of getting the support she needs. Worrying about tomorrow is like paying interest on money not yet borrowed. Teach consumers not to worry about the future, but to live and prepare for it one day at a time.

Only take a day's worth. When someone who has not felt good in years finally experiences stability and serenity, she may be gung ho to get her life back on track. A consumer who has not picked up a book in ten years suddenly decides that eighteen college credits, two NA meetings a day, a part-time job, and a battle to regain child custody ought to just about fill her schedule. She is suddenly trying to squeeze ten years of life into the next twenty-four hours. She is equally frustrated that she cannot get an advance on tomorrow. Soon her frustration turns to horror as she realizes she is "failing" again. Guess where she may turn for comfort?

Help her set realistic goals and decide how much closer she could reasonably expect to be to that goal twenty-four hours from now. Help her forget the rest of the work needed for that goal. She can work on her goals one day at a time, one day's worth at a time.

It will pass. Sometimes today is no day at the beach. But like most things, today will pass. Problems will pass, symptoms will pass, the urge to use alcohol and other drugs will pass. The trick is to get through the next twenty-four hours (or next hour) without picking up a drink or drug or doing something else that will make tomorrow worse. Tough times pass one day at a time.

Postpone that use. Another AA and NA slogan points out that *There is no problem so bad a drink or drug will not make it worse.* Teach consumers to put off using alcohol and other drugs. If a consumer cannot postpone using for twenty-four hours, ask her to wait one hour. At the end of an hour she can decide to wait another hour. She already knows she can go an hour without using because she has just done so. Many recovering addicts will tell how they got through tough times an hour or even five minutes at a time.

Serenity and sobriety are one day closer. Early recovery can be very difficult, but as time passes it gets easier. There is no way of knowing how much time has to pass. It's only known that things do get better one day at a time.

Savor today. Even on the worst of days something usually goes right. On good days it is easier to overlook all the pleasant experiences contained in a day. Teach consumers to savor each and every reward from sobriety. Clean clothes, somewhere to be, good coffee, and a good meal are all examples of rewards that are too often overlooked. Ask the consumers what is going well today. Even if it was the same thing that was going well yesterday, try to get them to appreciate it again today. Help consumers relearn to enjoy their lives one day at a time.

Hungry, Angry, Lonely, or Tired (HALT) and other slogans
Don't let yourself get too Hungry, Angry, Lonely, or Tired. Advise the consumer not to become too Hungry, Angry, Lonely, or Tired. Many consumers live on coffee, cigarettes, and junk food. They isolate themselves and experience sleep reversal (staying up all night, sleeping all day). Their lives have not gone the way they planned and they are understandably angry. The slogan HALT can help with their first steps in unraveling some of their negative emotions. Just improving nutrition and sleeping habits can make a world of difference.

CASE ILLUSTRATION 11: EASY DOES IT

Tina was a forty-five-year-old divorced mother of three. "Major depression" was listed as her primary diagnosis along with a note that her recurrent cocaine abuse may have been an attempt to self-medicate. All of her children were in foster care. She was hospitalized after her second suicide attempt. In ten years she had experimented with a variety of substances but preferred cocaine. After spending all of her inheritance on cocaine, she began to prostitute herself to obtain money for drugs. It was common for her to be hospitalized with severe depression after a cocaine binge. Prior to discharge she began meeting with outpatient and residential staff. She was eager to "get back to her life."

In formulating discharge goals, Tina listed staying clean, regaining custody of her children, obtaining a masters degree, finding a job, and buying a house. She attended NA meetings at the hospital but after two weeks reported that she had done all the Steps and felt no better. She could recite several of the slogans but did not see their relevance to her life.

Since, in this case, residential staff would spend more time with Tina than any other members of her treatment team, it was decided that the residential counselor would help Tina become more connected with NA. The counselor arranged to have meeting participation be part of Tina's agreement to live at the community residential program.

On her first day of treatment the counselor presented Tina with a meeting list and a quiz regarding slogans. When she could identify all the slogans on the sheet by their initials, he agreed to provide a gift certificate from a local store. They agreed that for the first thirty days her main goal was to wake up clean and go to bed clean. In that time she agreed to keep all appointments at the community mental health center and to attend one NA meeting per day. He agreed to either accompany her or provide transportation to each meeting if it was the first time she was attending.

By the third week she could identify all of the slogans. After the initial thirty days she was able to reevaluate her goals in light of what she had learned. Tina decided that getting a masters degree was not as important to her as getting her children back. She felt this fell under the slogan *Easy does it.* Still, school was important to her and she decided to take at least one class each semester: *But do it.* She also decided that she would not reach any of her goals if she returned to cocaine abuse: *First things first.*

Unfortunately, she would become depressed thinking about how long it might take to get her kids back and buy her own home. She and the residential counselor would discuss taking things *One day at a time.*

By three months slogans had become part of her automatic thinking. As she was discussing a problem she would talk about the slogan that applied. Sometimes her frustration would mount; still she stayed with the program.

Tina relapsed eighty-five days after she was released to the community residential rehab and ended up back in the hospital. Then she began attending NA again and remarked that she was starting over *One day at a time.* She put together one year of clean time.

The Point Is . . .

1. The slogans apply to many situations. They can help the consumer stay on track in recovery.
2. When consumers relapse, a knowledge of the slogans can help them start over and set realistic goals for themselves.

CHAPTER 9

———⬥———

TIMELINES AND DENIAL

Denial is an unconscious defense mechanism that prevents the consumer from seeing the severity of his substance abuse. It can be the biggest stumbling block in working with the consumer. While there is no easy way to address denial, a timeline can be very helpful (see page 116 for an example).

Use the information from the ongoing assessment to write a history of the consumer's involvement with institutions. In the far left column, list the dates when the consumer was hospitalized, jailed, involved with a child protective agency, left school, or was involved with some other institution. List the institution next to the dates and whenever possible, the location of those records.

Next to the institution, write a brief summary of what was going on when the consumer was involved with the institution. Print the letters *PPT* across the top to remind him of the slogan *People, places, and things.* Keep this summary as objective as possible. If the records show that the consumer had a blood alcohol level (BAL) of 0.15, list that empirical fact rather than writing that he was intoxicated. You do not *know* he was intoxicated, but you *do know* that his BAL was 0.15.

Sometimes the most objective data you have is fairly subjective—list it anyway. For example, if you have a police report that says the officer believed the consumer was drunk but that no tests were given, write "Police believed you were intoxicated." Do not list the consumer as having been drunk since you do not know that; you only know what the officer believed.

Being objective eliminates much of the arguing that can bog down an interview. Most consumers who abuse alcohol and other

111

drugs are adept at derailing discussions about their chemical use by dwelling on minute details. Whether or not a consumer was intoxicated on a given day in a twenty-year history of substance abuse can become a weeklong argument.

Next, list the substance used. Here again, write only what you know. If the use of cocaine was *suspected*, write "Cocaine, suspected" and a brief summary of why cocaine use was suspected.

Finally, list the consequences of the incident. This part of the timeline may change as the consumer's level of denial changes. He may later attribute consequences to drug use that he initially blamed on people or institutions. As his thinking clears, he may remember more about an incident.

When the timeline is completed, sit down with the consumer and review the role of substance abuse in his mental illness and other aspects of his life. If he still loves his chemical, the consumer may fight you every step of the way. He might attribute five straight hospitalizations, all of which occurred while using his favorite chemical, to coincidence: "Cocaine had nothing to do with it; it just happened that way." Often he will blame the hospitalizations on forces beyond his control: "It wasn't the booze; the hospital had a quota to meet." He may blame it on the people around him: "It's my mother's fault. She heard that people with schizophrenia shouldn't drink so she puts me away every time I do." He will miss the obvious. Having sold his couch and TV to buy crack he believes his problems stem from a lack of furniture: "You'd be depressed, too, if you had to sit on the floor and listen to the radio."

Do not expect the consumer in denial to say, "I see it all clearly now. Your insightful and detailed presentation has opened my eyes; I shall never use again. God bless you and the wonderful work you do."

More likely, the consumer will justify each event. Your job is to plow ahead, presenting the timeline as the reason you believe the consumer needs treatment, medications, and/or abstinence from all chemicals. Even if he dismisses all of the incidents, often a seed of doubt is planted and he may begin to see how substance abuse causes problems.

Some consumers know they have a problem. For them the timeline is a way of focusing on just how much damage they have done. It helps clear up fuzzy thinking and drive home the point that alcohol and other drugs are not helping them.

Review the timeline periodically. Add new information before the consumer has the opportunity to rationalize his substance abuse. For example, update the timeline the day after he is hospitalized. It is best to catch him while he is still hungover and clear that he was trying to kill himself. A week later he may write on his timeline that he "had a few beers and scratched my wrists to get attention."

A consumer may remember things differently as his thinking clears. Updating the timeline gives him a chance to reconsider some of the ways alcohol and other drugs have hurt him. He may decide that his first marriage never would have ended if he had taken his medications rather than smoked marijuana. Or he may decide he never would have married a drug dealer if he had not been abusing alcohol and other drugs. Both are a far cry from his initial belief that his marriage ended because of meddling from the police, child protection agencies, and the mental health system.

Reuniting an event with the original emotion is a primary reason for doing the timeline. When an event is tied to its original emotion, it becomes part of one's *personal history,* the realistic recall of life events. When divorced from the emotion, it becomes part of one's *personal mythology.* The subtle dishonesty of mythology enables a person to ignore the pain caused by substance use.

If a consumer laughs as he describes being trapped upside down in a car on a snowy highway ("I was so scared I almost wet myself. But two weeks later I was partying in my car again. It will take more than a little snow to kill me!"), he is not remembering emotionally what it was like. Divorced from the memory of the original emotion, the event becomes mythology.

If the same consumer had lost someone he loved, he could probably recall with great accuracy how he felt when he first heard of the death. Some of the old sadness would be reflected in the recall. The emotion is still tied to the event. Years later he can laugh about a moment he shared with his deceased friend, but some of the original sadness lingers on in remembering the death. For him the death is a real part of his personal history.

Your job is to help reunite a given event with its original emotions and to demythologize them. Ask the consumer how he felt at the time. Probe a little: What does he remember thinking? What did he say to himself immediately afterwards? Ask him to describe exactly what happened in as much detail as possible. Try to make the memory and the original emotion as vivid as possible. However, be careful not to use this technique with people who are decompensating, whether distraught or psychotic.

Remember, updating the timeline should be an ongoing process that records new events and new insights. Catch up with the consumer as soon as possible after a negative event and update the timeline then. Get it down on paper while it is still fresh in his mind.

CASE ILLUSTRATION 12: USING A TIMELINE

Suzanne is thirty-four years old and single. She has two children. Her son, Jamie, is seventeen and lives with foster parents. Suzanne has not seen him in several years. Her daughter, Alyssa, is five and lives with her father. Although Suzanne can visit Alyssa as often as she likes, she does not do so unless she is "really together"—she sees Alyssa about five times a year. Suzanne's assessment revealed that she has several goals that are incompatible with the use of alcohol and other drugs. Although she does not want custody of her children, Suzanne does want more contact. She is afraid, however, that her children will "misunderstand" her alcohol and other drug use. "There is a lot of government propaganda out there about booze and pills," she says. "My kids' respect is very important to me and I would not want them to get the wrong idea about me."

She would also like to go back to school. She has taken classes for her graduate equivalency degree but has dropped out twice because "the medications make me stupid." The first time she dropped out she was on Elavil; the second time, Prozac and Buspar.

Suzanne wants desperately to be free of her recurrent bouts of depression and anxiety. To her the term *normal* means "altogether free of depression." Unfortunately, she also considers using alcohol and other drugs part of being normal.

Following is part of her timeline and two excerpts from meetings with her counselor from the residential program where she lives. The first excerpt exemplifies the initial review of a timeline. Notice how the counselor does not argue with Suzanne, but merely presents the facts as she knows them.

Timeline

Name Suzanne

Date	Incident or Institution	Circumstances (People, Places, Things)	Used (Alcohol and Other Drugs)	Other Consequences
2/75	Expelled from high school	Vomited at school assembly program—drinking with friends	You reported being "wasted"	Forced out of school and into workforce uneducated
2/76	Admitted to County Memorial Hospital	Took more Valium than prescribed following the breakup of relationship	Toxicology report showed dangerous levels of Valium	30-day inpatient stay; mother called child welfare when pregnancy discovered
5/79	County Memorial Hospital	Arrested for being drunk and disorderly. Transferred from jail to hospital	Arresting officer reported you were intoxicated	Arrest record; 26-day hospital stay; lost your job
10/81	County Memorial Hospital	Took 10 times recommended dose of Benadryl	Toxic for Benadryl B.A.L.=0.19	35-day inpatient stay; not allowed to return to parents' home
11/81	County Memorial Hospital	Toxic levels of Elavil and alcohol in your bloodstream	Six pack of beer/all pills by your report	3 days on intensive care unit; 25 days in psychiatric hospital followed by 91 days at State Hospital
3/86	County jail	Possession of a controlled substance	???????	Probation; nobody willing to post your bail
7/90	City jail, County Memorial Hospital	Picked up by police after making threatening statement to kill yourself and your children	B.A.L.=0.27	Jamie heard of the incident; husband got a restraining order; 7 days in jail; inpatient stay in psychiatric hospital

(Excerpts from Suzanne's meetings with her counselor)

COUNSELOR: The first time you were hospitalized was in '76. You had Valium and alcohol in your bloodstream. Because of your pregnancy the hospital alerted child welfare.

SUZANNE: See what I mean? The baby wasn't even born yet and already they're saying I'm a bad mother. No one ever gives me a chance.

COUNSELOR: Hospital staff thought you had attempted suicide. They were also concerned about damage to the fetus.

SUZANNE: I got confused. I had a little wine and I forgot how many pills I had taken. It was an honest mistake. You ever make a mistake? You ever have a glass of wine?

COUNSELOR: That was right after Jamie's father took off. So there you are, seventeen, pregnant, out of school, and depressed. This was one of those times you told me about when you want to have a few just to get away, right?

SUZANNE: I was scared to death. I needed a break.

COUNSELOR: A few beers may have seemed like the answer, but what were the results?

SUZANNE: As always, my mother freaked, which freaked the doctors, and instead of letting me sleep it off they locked me in County in Memorium.

COUNSELOR: According to the records you had a seizure. You were hospitalized for thirty days and, as you said, child welfare was involved before the baby was even born. Going into the hospital you were still depressed—you didn't really get a break. Jamie's father was still gone.

> SUZANNE: You really get a kick out of rubbing this in don't you?
>
> COUNSELOR: Not at all. I was just thinking out loud how terrible your life must have felt before you took that first drink. Then as you're trying to find some peace, the sky falls in. It's like that slogan, *There is no problem so bad a drink or a drug won't make it worse.*
>
> SUZANNE: Lots of people drink when they're down, but you don't see them getting thrown in the hospital.
>
> COUNSELOR: That may be true. All I know for sure is that when you drink, bad things happen to you. I'm betting that if you don't drink, your life will get a whole lot better.

Notice that the counselor presents the facts without confusing what was known with what was believed. She never says Suzanne was drunk or suicidal. She quotes records and sticks to the recorded facts. The counselor states that the hospital staff believed she had made a suicide attempt. It is a fact that staff believed this. Whether or not she really tried to kill herself is not known.

The counselor allows that Suzanne's life may have looked bleak at the time, but things only got worse with alcohol. Suzanne treats the whole episode as an error in judgment, thinking a drink would make the situation more bearable. Instead, it made the situation much worse. The counselor uses the information to point out the error in judgment and its consequences.

Never does the counselor imply that Suzanne is a bad person. There is no moral judgment in anything she says to Suzanne. For example, she never comments on whether child welfare should have been called. She simply points out that they were called and that alcohol played some role in their intervention.

Here is the rest of the conversation:

COUNSELOR: So in '90 you had a blood alcohol level of 0.27. You were picked up by the police in front of your ex-husband's house.

SUZANNE: It's not enough for him that he has Alyssa—he has to put me in jail to feel like a man.

COUNSELOR: The police report said you threatened to set his house on fire.

SUZANNE: What bullshit. I was just trying to scare him. He knew it too. But once you are labeled as crazy, they lock you up every chance they get. You know he smokes in bed? I make one threat that I would never carry out and off I go to the hospital. He drinks beer and falls asleep with a cigarette in his mouth, and he's allowed to have custody. He's the one who's a threat to Alyssa's welfare.

COUNSELOR: You were taken to the hospital. Your husband got a restraining order and told Alyssa what had happened. He also got in touch with child welfare who warned Jamie's foster parents. When I visited you in the hospital, you were crying because you did not think Alyssa and Jamie would understand.

SUZANNE: They line up to kick you when you're down. Now my kids think I'm a lunatic, thanks to that bastard.

COUNSELOR: When the police picked you up you had a BAL of 0.27.

SUZANNE: I never should have been picked up in the first place.

COUNSELOR: The people you believe are "out to get you" always seem to "get you" when you're drinking. I wonder how much trouble you could avoid if you didn't drink.

SUZANNE: I never drink in front of my kids. None of this would have happened if he hadn't called the police. It's not the booze; it's that idiot I married. Everybody drinks but you don't see their ex's throwing them into the hospital.

COUNSELOR: Still your children did hear about the episode even if you don't drink in front of them. That may work against your goal of spending more time with them and gaining their respect. That must be hard on you. I wish they could see you on the days you're sober, when things are going well.

Again, the counselor does not argue with Suzanne about whether she deserved to be hospitalized. She merely states what happened and how it hinders Suzanne's efforts to reach her goals. The counselor points out that alcohol played a role in her difficulties.

The counselor does not wait for Suzanne to say, "Aha! Your insightful presentation has opened my eyes. I shall never use again!" She accepts that Suzanne, in denial, will rationalize her use of alcohol and other drugs. She simply continues presenting the facts, planting the seeds of recovery, hoping that in an enlightened moment Suzanne will see that alcohol is a big part of her problem.

Someone coping with a mental illness may have numerous events to list on the timeline. List them anyway. Sometimes a timeline's sheer length impresses upon a consumer how much has been lost as a result of alcohol and other drug use, and how many years have passed since the first loss.

It is common for a consumer to dwell not on what happened, but on whether or not he was treated fairly by friends, family, and the authorities. After being hospitalized he may want to argue about the grounds used to commit him. He may believe that the people around him harbor ulterior motives for hospitalizing him.

Your first reaction may be to argue with him. You may find yourself in the position of defending other people's actions—of saying whether or not the consumer deserved to be arrested, hospitalized, expelled, denied custody, divorced, or sued. However, this can bog down the review, and in the consumer's eyes it can put you firmly in the enemy camp: "I can't believe you're siding with them!"

Stressing vulnerability may be more effective. Show the consumer that most of his problems occur when he is using alcohol and other drugs. For some reason he seems to be most vulnerable then. If possible use statistics, such as citing the percentage of people in jail who were arrested while using alcohol and other drugs. Emphasize that people with a mental illness who use alcohol and other drugs are far more likely to be hospitalized than those who do not use.

The consumer may realize that people with a mental illness are more vulnerable to the effects of alcohol and other drugs and then decide to quit using. Alternatively, he may decide that it is easier for the authorities to persecute the mentally ill when they are using alcohol and other drugs. In the end, however, it does not matter if he stops using because he has seen the light or because he wants to avoid run-ins with the authorities.

Suzanne's case illustrates how to use the timeline for a consumer who is not doing well. But the timeline can also be used for someone who is working on recovery. Every positive event or any progress toward the consumer's goals can be documented on the timeline. The steps are the same whether the event is negative or positive. The difference is that the focus is on how recovery made the event possible.

CHAPTER 10

CONTINGENCY CARDS

Contingency cards are action plans written on index cards to help the consumer "in case of an emergency." They can be created for a single event, a day, a week, or for long-term problems. The cards allow the counselor and the consumer to plan for difficult situations, for example:

- Friends offering the consumer substances
- AA or NA members questioning the consumer's need for medications
- Waiting for public transportation near a bar or where drugs are sold
- Flare-up of psychiatric symptoms
- Check day
- Painful anniversaries
- Feeling angry
- Feeling bored
- Feeling depressed
- Feeling lonely

On one side of the card, help the consumer list all the people that she can call if she encounters any of the problems on the list, for example:

- *Clinician's phone number:* This should include paging instructions and the phone numbers of other staff who can be called in case the clinician is unavailable. The consumer may be standing at a pay phone in front of a bar—it is vital that she be able to reach someone.

- *Sponsor's phone number:* Sometimes consumers are hesitant to call their sponsors. It's a good idea for the consumer to arrange times in advance when it is okay to call the sponsor.
- *Other recovering people:* As consumers attend more Twelve Step meetings, they should be encouraged to get as many phone numbers as possible. Many recovering people will not hesitate in giving out their number because they view it as part of Twelfth Step work.
- *Clergy*
- *Family members*
- *Friends*

Warning

Before adding anyone's number to the list, be certain that the person is supportive of the consumer being abstinent from chemicals and compliant with medications!

On the other side of the card, help the consumer develop a plan of action that spells out how she will handle threatening situations. A general plan includes situations the consumer faces frequently. A more specific plan might include an hour-by-hour description of how the consumer will get through a particularly stressful situation or day. Examples of both follow, and treatment recommendations are discussed throughout the book. It helps to tailor the plan to the consumer.

Complete a contingency card as part of a planning session. Make sure the card is a collaborative effort. The consumer must agree to call the people listed or the card is meaningless.

Here is a sample daily card for Ralph, someone who has relapsed several times.

(Front of sample card)

Staff member:	555-4397
Her back-up or on-call:	555-1414
	or 555-8210
Another drug and alcohol clinician:	555-2211
Alcoholics Anonymous:	555-3744
Narcotics Anonymous:	555-2990
Dial-a-sober thought:	555-1615
Dad:	555-7021

*I agree to call at least three of these numbers
if I feel like using or going off meds.*

On the front of his card, Ralph lists people he can call. Make sure he is able to reach someone. You do not want him being put on hold and getting frustrated. He may know all too well how he wants to deal with frustration.

(Back of sample card)

1. Downtown waiting for the bus craving alcohol
   a. I will call my clinician
   b. I will go get a cup of coffee
   c. I will go to the recovery center

2. People at Mom's are drinking
   a. I will leave and go to an AA meeting
   b. I will call Dad to see if I can visit him

On the back of the card are two situations that Ralph fears. He decided ahead of time what to do if he is in a situation that might contribute to a relapse. One weakness in Ralph's card is item 2a because he may not know where a meeting is being held (but he knows where a bar is open). A more thoroughly prepared card might list the meetings being held that day, including times and locations.

CHAPTER 11

———

TWELVE STEP PROGRAMS

Not getting lost on the road to recovery

As a clinician, one of the worst things you can do for the person coping with mental illness and substance abuse is to give him an Alcoholics Anonymous or Narcotics Anonymous meeting list and send him on his way. Many negative things can occur.

He may get lost on his way to the meeting and return to familiar haunts. He may go to the wrong church basement. (One man went to the wrong church while looking for an AA meeting and stumbled into an Octoberfest celebration, complete with kegs of beer.) If he does get lost in a strange neighborhood, is he more likely to stumble across the local library or an open bar?

Once at the meeting, he may feel overwhelmed. One consumer fled in terror when "one of those NA guys came at me with his arms out like some kinda zombie." No one had told him that many NA meetings have greeters who hug people arriving for the meeting.

Depending on symptoms, he may feel uncomfortable in large groups, small groups, discussion meetings, speaker meetings, or rooms with few exits. He may not know what is appropriate behavior at Twelve Step meetings. What should he say if he does not want to speak? Is it okay to leave early? What about mentioning being on medications? If unprepared, he may feel awkward and therefore be less likely to return.

Observing Twelve Step Meetings

Consumers are not the only ones who may not know what is appropriate at AA and NA meetings. Many university addiction courses require students to observe one or more Twelve Step meeting. Too often students bring notebooks, even tape recorders. When this happens, the chairperson of the meeting is forced to ask the student to leave those items outside.

Get a meeting list by calling the local AA, NA, or other group office. Some meetings will be listed as open. "Open" Twelve Step meetings can be observed. Go to meetings, and when you get there grab a cup of coffee, sit back, and relax. What you hear is so simple, yet has such great impact that you will not be able to forget it.

What about after the meeting? He may get through the meeting but find himself sorely tempted as he waits at the next bus stop across from a rowdy bar. Many people have lost their sobriety by stopping at a bar for a soda when they were trying to get out of the rain or snow.

The Point Is . . .

Merely handing a consumer a list of local Twelve Step meetings is not sufficient.

A better way

There are several offshoots of the Twelve Step program for people with mental illness and substance abuse. Several of these groups have revised the Twelve Steps to include addiction, medications, and self-help. You can also adapt these steps to your clinical population and run an in-house meeting based on your adaptation. (See Appendix II, pages 161–165 for the Steps of various programs.)

Adapt and teach the traditions of Alcoholics Anonymous and Narcotics Anonymous. Knowing the traditions makes it easier for consumers to fit in at Twelve Step meetings in the community. (A copy is found in the appendixes.)

There are several ways to expose consumers to self-help programs. Here are some methods listed according to descending staff involvement:

- *In-house, on-site, "practice" meeting, based loosely on a Twelve Step program, run by staff.* Using your adaptation of the Steps, hold an on-site meeting in your facility just for consumers in your program (in-house). It helps to use the Alcoholics Anonymous and Narcotics Anonymous format, but be flexible. Stop the meeting to allow for questions about how things are done at community-based AA and NA meetings. When someone behaves inappropriately, talking out of turn for example, ask the group how the situation might be handled in a "real" AA or NA meeting. Better yet, ask the group how *they* want to handle the situation. The idea is to provide a group within the safety of the clinic that teaches consumers how to use the Twelve Step programs. Consumers can use this meeting to practice for outside meetings, as an alternative to outside meetings, or to discuss experiences at community meetings.

- *In-house, on-site meetings, run by members of the Twelve Step recovery community.* This meeting is held in your facility by members of AA, NA, and other recovery groups. Many of these groups consider outreach part of their recovery and will be willing to volunteer. AA and NA have hospital and institution committees as well as written guidelines for volunteering at treatment facilities. Familiarize yourself with these guidelines and discuss any other expectations you have with the volunteers. The advantage of having Twelve Step members run the meeting is that it gives consumers contact with recovering individuals without having to go out to meetings in the community.

- *On-site meetings open to the public.* Members of Twelve Step groups hold meetings that are "open" to the community at your facility. This arrangement allows consumers to experience a community-based Twelve Step meeting on "home turf." Holding the meeting when consumers are in the building increases the chances that a group can attend the meeting together.

- *AA and NA meetings in the community.* This allows consumers to get away from your facility and provides an opportunity to apply what they have learned in the in-house groups.

By this time, you have probably followed the suggestion in chapter 4 to attend a Twelve Step meeting. But if not, be sure to attend an AA or NA meeting before holding an in-house meeting. Many Twelve Step meetings are open to the public. All they ask is that anything heard at the meeting is not repeated. It is a small price for all that may be gained.

If you feel compelled to tell every third person at a Twelve Step meeting that you are only there to observe, you are probably feeling the stigma. Look closely and you will notice most of the members are not embarrassed. They have gotten past the stigma. Keep this in mind when a consumer initially resists going to meetings.

Try to learn how leaderless groups of recovering addicts can be such powerful forces for recovery. The more you know about recovery, the easier it will be to design a program that addresses mental illness and addiction. At the very least, know the Twelve Steps, the Twelve Traditions, the types of meetings, and how the meetings are conducted. In this way, you will know how to answer questions like "Is NA a cult?" or "Won't I get addicted to AA meetings?"

Consumers who decide to attend community meetings need to consider several issues:

- *Where is the meeting?* How does she get there and how does she get home? Will there be any time before or after the meeting when the consumer will be stuck somewhere with nothing to do? (The two biggest calamities to strike a newly sober consumer are time on her hands and money in her pocket.)

- *What type of meeting is it?* Some people are more comfortable at speaker meetings. Others prefer discussion meetings or Step meetings (in which one of the Twelve Steps is discussed).
- *How accepting is this meeting?* How do group members treat people who are different, such as those with mental illness?
- *Where are the exits?* How easy is it for the anxious consumer to leave? (People who are anxious about community meetings can go to speaker meetings and sit by an exit. If they feel uncomfortable, they can leave without causing a commotion.)

Warning

Alcohol and other drug abuse mimics mental illness. Many people in AA and NA have been misdiagnosed and placed on psychotropic medication. Once clean and sober, they found they no longer needed the medication. When the consumer tells such individuals that she has been diagnosed as suffering from depression and takes Elavil, it is not surprising that the AA or NA member tells her to get off the medication: "That's what they said about me, but I've been off the meds *and* the sauce for ten years!" You can help consumers feel comfortable about taking medications by explaining their diagnosis and the rationale for medications and by rehearsing how to deal with pressure to stop taking medications. If someone at a meeting is persistent about stopping psychotropic medications, we ask the consumer to give that person a copy of *The A.A. Member: Medications and Other Drugs* (Alcoholics Anonymous 1984). This pamphlet explains that no AA member is to play doctor and that some people require medications.

The recovery network

The recovery network is the group of people the consumer knows who are also in recovery. At most Twelve Step meetings new members are encouraged to get the phone numbers of people willing to talk to them when they are in distress or have questions about recovery. The recovery network replaces the social group that the consumer abused alcohol and other drugs with. The more people involved in the consumer's recovery network, the better (provided that these people understand the need for the consumer to be on psychotropic medication).

Counselors should do everything possible to help the consumer develop the list of recovering people he knows. Realistically evaluate his efforts to expand his recovery network. Do not, for example, expect a very paranoid consumer to approach many strangers about his recovery. Help him evaluate his list of contacts. If every person in his recovery network is a woman he is attracted to, help him reassess his reasons for contacting these women.

Ask the consumer to test the recovery network *before* he feels he needs to. Some consumers are skeptical that anyone would be willing to talk with them about their problems with mental illness and substance abuse. Calling *before* a crisis arises reassures the consumer that somebody will be there when he needs help.

Some consumers may be prone to abuse the system by calling continuously and asking for inappropriate help. It is best to set limits early, defining when to call and what is appropriate to expect from a member of a recovery network.

CHAPTER 12

———⋙⋘———

GROUP TREATMENT APPROACHES

A variety of group treatment approaches can be used to help consumers recover. Groups provide a number of advantages to consumers, such as opportunities to

- Learn more about their illnesses and the recovery process
- Share problems, concerns, and struggles, as well as hope, strength, and success
- Give and receive support with other consumers
- Develop skills to recover from their illnesses

When combined with individual and family sessions, medications, and self-help programs, group treatment provides consumers with a comprehensive treatment program.

Interventions of group leaders

Group leaders use a variety of interventions, depending on the type of group conducted and the level of consumer participation. Both the content of discussion and the process of group interaction are important parts of recovery groups. In general, the leaders need to maintain balance among three elements: the individual members, the group as a whole, and the topic or problem being discussed.

Provide specific information about mental illness, addiction, and the recovery process. You may be amazed at how little "street smart" consumers know about these topics. Make sure the information relates to their life. Do not tell them about the neurotransmitter system. Tell them about stability and serenity. Show them in practical terms how they can make their lives better.

Keep the group discussion moving and make sure you cover the material in psychoeducational groups. Some group members will want to talk about everything but recovery. Others will want to discuss a personal issue each week, every week, until every group member who is not court-committed to attend will drop out. Keep the group on task. It helps to agree at the start of group what you will cover that day. Anything off the topic should not be ignored; rather it should be referred to another group or to an individual session.

Involve as many consumers in the group discussions as possible by discussing episodes of substance use or "close calls." The quiet consumer can at least report on her progress. She may not want to discuss that day's topic, but she can report any major changes in psychiatric symptoms and her attendance at self-help programs for addiction, mental illness, or both.

Heap encouragement on the consumer who attends self-help programs. Everyone likes a pat on the back. You have no way of knowing if anyone else in the consumer's life cheers her efforts. Praise from you and the group members may help keep her going to Twelve Step programs.

Model healthy interpersonal behaviors but challenge inappropriate behaviors and negative attitudes. Set a positive example by the way you interact with people. Show the consumer how to express herself appropriately. If you explode every time someone is late for group, consumers may learn an unproductive way of dealing with anger. Ignoring the latecomer's tardiness teaches the consumer that you do not value the group enough to insist on punctual attendance. Addressing lateness openly and rationally models appropriate behavior. Hopefully the consumer will apply your example to her own interactions.

Help group members challenge inappropriate behavior and negative attitudes. Group members always outnumber group leaders. Collectively, group members hold more clout—it is, after all, their group. With your guidance, let group members decide what will and will not be tolerated in their group.

Help group members talk directly to each other to give feedback, share support, and solve problems. Group members are the ones who have the most in common with each other. Let them help each other as much as possible. If a group member talks to you each time she speaks, other group members will feel excluded. Picture yourself sitting in someone's office while she takes five calls over the speakerphone before talking to you. You hear five personal conversations but have no input, no chance to help the person on the other end of the phone. If the five conversations last long enough, you may lose interest or feel that the person you are sitting with is too busy to help you.

Now picture yourself sitting in a conference room with five animated people. Each of the five people has had similar experiences and struggles with recovery as you do. They all talk to each other and to you, offering advice, comfort, and appropriate confrontation. Similarly, the group where consumers interact is usually much more appealing than the group where everyone talks only to the staff member.

Encourage everyone to share ideas and experiences. Members who talk too much and dominate will have to be controlled so that quieter members have an opportunity to share. Quiet members often have to be gently drawn into the discussion by being directly asked what they think about or how they relate to a specific issue being discussed.

Develop "rituals" for conducting groups. For example, prior to starting a group discussion, ask each member to introduce herself, and then ask if any member has used alcohol or other drugs since the last meeting or has had any "close calls" or strong cravings. Or, prior to ending the group, ask the members to briefly state one point from the meeting that was most meaningful to them and to state their plan for recovery for the next week.

Psychoeducational groups

Psychoeducational groups are based on the assumption that providing information about mental illness and substance abuse helps consumers begin recovery. Consumers learn coping skills to deal with common problems in recovery from both illnesses. They learn enough to make informed decisions about their recovery, treatment, and addiction.

Using a discussion format, the groups focus on a specific recovery topic with objectives (Daley and Thase in press, 72–74). Usually, a specific group session has three to five objectives for the topic. The main methods of conducting psychoeducational group sessions include lectures, discussions, videotapes, readings of recovery literature, role plays, and answering questions in recovery workbooks. Sessions typically last from forty-five to ninety minutes depending on who attends group; for example, restless consumers benefit from briefer sessions. Information is provided to consumers by the group leaders, but there is also much interaction among consumers who share personal experiences and ask questions about the topic.

Although psychoeducational groups provide plenty of opportunities for consumers to share personal problems, it is important to cover the planned material and avoid open-ended discussions. There will always be important issues or problems that consumers wish to discuss, but failing to cover the group's curriculum defeats the group's purpose. If you believe a group member is in great distress or decompensating, see this member after the group or encourage him to contact a member of his treatment team for an individual crisis session.

Group Topics. The following list of discussion topics can be developed easily into psychoeducational group sessions. Some sessions focus more on substance abuse issues and others focus more on psychiatric issues. Whenever possible relate the topic to both types of disorders. Stress the effects of each disorder on the other.

Some topics can be covered in one session; some need multiple sessions. For example, coping with anger or depression requires several sessions to allow for in-depth coverage. However, the number of sessions spent on each topic, and which topics are covered, depends on the time available. If you only have time to conduct eight sessions, then choose the eight most relevant ones from this list. Tailor the topics to the group's needs. If, for example, three of ten group members are crying openly, you may want to address coping with sadness.

Possible group topics include

- Understanding substance abuse and addiction (signs and symptoms, etiology, and effects)
- Understanding chronic mental illness or specific types of psychiatric disorders (signs and symptoms, etiology, and effects)
- Understanding denial and other defense mechanisms
- Effects of illness on self and others (medical, interpersonal, emotional, legal, occupational, financial, and spiritual)
- Understanding alcohol (medical and psychosocial effects)
- Understanding crack and cocaine (medical and psychosocial effects)
- Understanding marijuana (medical and psychosocial effects)
- Understanding other chemicals (medical and psychosocial effects)
- The recovery process and keys to successful recovery for consumers
- Phases of recovery for consumers
- Dealing with high-risk people, places, and things
- Coping with urges and cravings to use alcohol or other drugs
- Surviving check day and coping with pressures to give away money
- Refusing offers to use alcohol or other drugs
- Dealing with pressures to get off medications
- Developing structure and routine

- Coping with persistent symptoms of mental illness
- Coping with feelings
- Coping with anger
- Coping with anxiety
- Coping with boredom
- Coping with depression
- Coping with loneliness
- Coping with guilt and shame
- Sexuality and recovery
- Impact of disorders on family and significant relationships
- Using self-help programs and recovery clubs
- Developing a recovery network
- Spirituality in recovery
- Changing negative thinking
- Coping with character defects or personality problems
- Coping with lapses to alcohol and other drug use
- Understanding relapse to addiction (risk factors, warning signs, and relapse prevention strategies)
- Relapse of psychiatric illness (risk factors, warning signs, and relapse prevention strategies)

Other more specialized topics can easily be developed for use in psychoeducational groups according to the needs and interests of consumers (e.g., financial issues in recovery, increasing assertiveness).

Possible structure of psychoeducational group sessions
A specific format helps group members know what to expect and what is expected of them. What follows is an outline of a typical psychoeducational group session.

Introduction. Each group member states her name and why she is in the group. Some groups have members say how long they have been clean. For example, "My name is Susan. I'm here to learn about cocaine, which was always my drug of choice. Hold on to your seats 'cause I haven't used any for three straight weeks now!"

This part of the group is a good time to check on group members' progress. It is a time to applaud consumers for efforts made and hurdles jumped. The introductory phase helps bring the group members closer together.

Agenda. Set goals for the group. What do you, as a leader, and the group want to accomplish in the next forty-five to ninety minutes? Collaborate with the consumers to pick the most relevant aspects of a topic. For example, if the topic for the day is "cocaine," you might decide to discuss just the biological effects of cocaine for the first half of the group. Be as specific as discussing how it affects the heart, lungs, and brain, leaving other organs for next week. Or discuss cocaine more generally, using one group session to cover cocaine's social and psychological effects. But whatever is agreed to, make every effort to cover that material in group.

Having an agenda makes it easier to redirect consumers who want to discuss issues other than that day's topic. Recognize the importance of the consumer's issue, but find another more appropriate place for her to discuss it.

Presentation. This is the core of the discussion. The group leader presents material for the group's consideration. It helps to introduce the topic with a question. You might ask any of the following questions:

- "Why do they put that label on your medications 'do not mix with alcohol'?"
- "What is the first thing you should do when you start to crave alcohol and other drugs?"
- "Why do we call some chemicals 'medications' and others 'drugs'?"
- "Why shouldn't people who are depressed drink?"

The idea is to have consumers provide as much information as they know and for you to correct misperceptions and fill in the gaps. If you ask a group how HIV is spread, expect a variety of responses. Many of the group members will know that sharing needles and unprotected sex can spread HIV. Some group members may believe that HIV is spread by contact with public toilet seats and drinking fountains. Still others will not know what is meant by "safe sex."

Summary. During the last ten to fifteen minutes review what was covered in group. It helps to have group members state three to five key points. Then you can ask group members to agree to return for the next group. It may help to assign homework for the next session.

Problem-solving groups

Problem-solving groups are open-ended discussion groups in which members share mutual problems and explore coping strategies. Tailor the discussion in these groups to the needs and issues of the particular group. Topics include substance abuse, mental illness, and other important areas of the consumer's life.

The main goal of a problem-solving group is to provide mechanisms for consumers to help each other identify and explore problems and solutions. Consumers give each other feedback during group sessions and provide additional strategies to cope with specific problems. These groups are best suited for consumers who have established several months of sobriety, although lapses and relapses do occur and need to be discussed in group sessions.

Following is a brief review of typical pitfalls encountered in problem-solving groups and ways you can deal with them.

Too much time spent on discussing the problem and not enough time spent on discussing coping strategies. This pitfall can be avoided by asking group members to be brief and succinct in presenting specific problems and to avoid long-winded "war stories" of drug or alcohol use. Also encourage members to discuss alternative ways of coping with the problems presented in group.

A group member is needy and always seems to have a pressing problem to discuss. This pitfall can be dealt with by commenting on what is observed in the group process, such as "I've noticed that during the past two group sessions we have focused only on Paul's problems. Other group members seemed hesitant to bring up their problems. What does the group think about this?" You may also want to help members prioritize who will present problems during a given group meeting or suggest a specific group member take time during a group meeting to discuss a problem.

A group member never seems to have any problems to discuss in the group. This pitfall can be addressed by asking this member to identify something he wants to change in himself or his life.

Members may come late for the group session. It helps to have the group establish its own policy on lateness. For example, a group may decide that no one will be admitted after a certain time for any reason. When someone arrives late, it is usually the group members who remind him of the group's policy.

CHAPTER 13

---※---

WORKING WITH THE CONSUMER'S FAMILY

Mental illness and substance abuse affect families in a variety of ways. Family members of consumers commonly experience fear, anxiety, anger, worry, and disappointment. The emotional and financial burden for families varies from mild to extreme.

The specific effects on a given family depend on the nature of the consumer's illnesses, her behavior, and the family's coping abilities and support systems. For example, despite her problems with depression and alcoholism, Belinda always managed to hold a good job and take care of her children. She tried hard to meet her children's needs, even when depression sapped her energy. Although affected in some ways by her disorders, her kids did relatively well in school and in the community.

Frank, on the other hand, has created havoc with his family. He has been in and out of mental hospitals, detoxification centers, and jails too many times to count. When he takes his medications and complies with treatment, he usually does fairly well. But he often stops medications and treatment to go on alcohol and cocaine binges. Frank's family is burned out and tired. It breaks his mother's heart to see him decompensate and end up in an institution time after time. His father believes that Frank will never get better if he doesn't stop abusing drugs.

Involving the family in assessment and treatment often helps. But sometimes, unfortunately, the consumer is totally alienated from her family or the family simply wants to be left alone. And there may be times in which other serious family problems make it difficult or impossible for them to engage in treatment. Be realistic about what you can and cannot do to help a family. There will, however, be many cases in which you can work with the family.

Practical family-related interventions

The following brief descriptions are some ways you can help the consumer improve his relationship with his family and some ways to work directly with him and his family together. Remember, you do not have to be a family therapist to help the family of a consumer.

Help the consumer understand how addiction and mental illness, alone or in combination, commonly affect the family or individual members. General information on the effects of illness on the family makes it easier for the consumer to take a more personal look at how his family may have been affected. You can provide this information through group treatment sessions and through literature on mental illness, substance abuse, and the family.

Help the consumer take a personal look at the specific effects of his behavior and illnesses on his family. Help the consumer identify how his family was affected by either or both of his illnesses. He may feel guilty and shameful—these are normal reactions when examining oneself and one's impact on others. Be prepared for him to deny or minimize his impact on the family or to avoid discussing this issue. Be prepared to help him understand and work through these feelings.

Encourage the consumer to involve his family in assessment and treatment sessions. Unless there is some legitimate reason to exclude the family from treatment, set the expectation early that working with the family is an important part of the treatment process. Families can provide helpful information during the initial assessment process and during the course of treatment. Seeing the consumer and family together also gives you a better understanding of how they interact. If you believe family therapy is needed in addition to education and support, and you are not trained to conduct family therapy yourself, help the consumer and his family find a family therapist, preferably in your own agency or clinic. Typically, when treatment is splintered, the consumer can more easily play one professional against the other.

If the consumer is unsure what to say or how to approach his family, discuss how he can feel more comfortable and confident engaging his family in sessions. If necessary, use role plays to teach the consumer skills to use in asking his family to participate. If this does not work, you can ask the consumer's permission to talk directly to his family and then invite them for a family meeting.

Offer family psychoeducational programs. Educational programs can be offered on a regular or periodic basis to provide families with information and to teach them strategies to cope with mental illness and substance abuse. A variety of formats can be used, such as a half-day or full-day psychoeducational workshop with several families, or ongoing programs (weekly, biweekly, or monthly). In addition to acquiring information and learning coping skills, families can offer each other support by sharing their strength and hope. Educating families about illness and recovery empowers them; teaching them practical coping strategies reduces their burden and enables them to learn new ways of dealing with their loved one. The end of this chapter offers a sample family psychoeducational workshop format.

Encourage families to share their feelings and concerns; ask them questions about mental illness and substance abuse. Families need to be given a chance to share their questions and concerns about their loved one. The most common concerns and questions of families of consumers include

- What are the diagnoses and what caused the illnesses in the first place?
- How can treatment help, how long will it last, and what can we expect from it?

- How long will my loved one have to take medications? What might happen if he mixes alcohol or street drugs with his psychiatric medications?
- What can we do to help support his recovery without always worrying, "walking on eggshells," or feeling responsible for him?
- How should we deal with intoxication, severe mood swings, psychotic symptoms, threats of suicide or actual attempts, threats of violence or actual violent episodes?
- What should we do when he abruptly stops treatment or stops taking his psychotropic medications?
- In what circumstances should we contact the doctor or therapist to discuss concerns over changes in his behavior?
- How can we deal with our feelings of responsibility, anger, guilt, desperation, or disappointment?
- Are other family members vulnerable to developing an addiction or mental health disorder?
- Should we drink alcohol in front of our loved one? Will this tempt him to drink?

Hearing these concerns expressed by his own or others' families often makes the consumer more aware of the experience of his family and what it feels like for them. He learns that his actions affect everyone, not just himself. He learns that others care about him but are often bewildered about what to do.

Encourage the consumer and family to attend self-help groups. Attending self-help groups with the consumer can help the family better understand illness and recovery. Families also benefit from attending their own specific meetings such as Al-Anon or Naranon for addiction, or family-focused mental health support groups. Providing information on self-help meetings, answering questions, and encouraging attendance are very valuable services for families. (It also helps to have literature on self-help programs in your clinic waiting area.)

Encourage the consumer and family to talk directly to each other about the mental illness, substance abuse, and their effects on the family. This is best accomplished after the consumer and family have had an opportunity to gain information and attend family psychoeducational programs and self-help meetings. The consumer should be prepared to hear some things he may find unpleasant. The purpose is not to make the consumer feel bad, although this may result from such a discussion, but to initiate an ongoing dialogue between the consumer and his family so that issues and feelings are shared and discussed openly.

Encourage the consumer to use the "making amends" Steps of the Twelve Step program (Steps 8 and 9). Practicing these Steps is an excellent way for the consumer to begin undoing damage caused by the illnesses. Be careful, however, not to rush him into this too quickly, as it can be emotionally overwhelming. Some period of sobriety and psychiatric stability is needed before he should make amends. However, inviting family members to treatment sessions or support group meetings, followed by a discussion of recovery issues, is an indirect way to start the amends process.

Encourage the family to stop "enabling." Enabling behaviors reduce the likelihood that the consumer will see how his behavior leads to problems. Enabling gives him the message that someone else will cover up or pick up the pieces if he gets in trouble due to drinking, drugging, or acting irresponsibly. Two examples of enabling are (1) shielding him from the consequences of his alcohol or other drug use by bailing him out of trouble and (2) not holding him accountable for his actions, or taking over his responsibilities. For example, Dave experienced schizophrenia and substance abuse. His parents paid many fines and often paid his rent and bought him food, even though he spent most of his money on alcohol and other drugs. Although they had good intentions, Dave's parents gave him the message "Don't worry if you get in trouble with the law or get in a financial mess; Mom and Dad will make things better for you."

Until his parents stopped enabling, Dave had little incentive to take a serious look at his addiction and how it led to trouble with the law and with meeting his financial responsibilities.

Guidelines for working with families

Although there is much more to learn about working with families, the following guidelines provide a basic list of "do's" and "don'ts" (Daley and Thase in press, 62–63).

Avoid labeling the family. See the family as your ally and avoid labeling them as "sick," "dysfunctional," or "codependent." The family is not the client and despite their problems and limitations, they know the consumer much better than you do. This is not to say there is no dysfunction in families. But labeling the dysfunction often leads to making judgments that may influence your work with the family. For example, if you believe a family is hopeless because of its chronic problems, you are likely to give up quickly and assume you cannot do much to help them.

Engage the family early. The sooner contact is made with the family, the greater the likelihood they can be engaged in treatment. An excellent strategy is to invite the family to the initial assessment. When contacting the family, tell them their help is needed to better understand and work with their family member. Emphasize that their input is important to the treatment team. It helps to view the engagement process as being equally important as the treatment process because if you can't engage families, they won't benefit from the services you have to offer. Be persistent and remember it may take more than one attempt to get a family involved.

Be accessible to families. Offer evening or weekend appointments if needed, especially for working family members. Also, return the family's phone calls promptly and make sure they can reach you easily—whether to ask a question or tell you of a significant change in the functioning of their loved one.

Offer direct advice. If family members ask you how to cope with a particular situation, help them identify options. Give them direct advice on handling difficult situations. For example, if a consumer suddenly stops attending treatment and self-help meetings, advise the family to sit down and openly discuss their concerns and insist the consumer resume treatment. If she gets drunk or high and tries to antagonize a family member by arguing, advise the family to avoid arguments while she is intoxicated and then to confront her when she is sober.

Focus on family strengths. Remember, many families have coped with difficult situations for years and have developed good survival strategies. Don't focus solely on family problems and forget their strengths. If a family or individual member does something well, give them positive reinforcement by acknowledging their behavior.

Provide a realistic view of treatment and recovery. It is important to give the message that *everyone can get better in some ways,* even people who have been chronically ill. In some instances, however, providing a realistic view of treatment may mean helping the family accept that their family member will always have to live with some symptoms and limitations imposed by the illnesses, especially in cases of persistent psychiatric illness. In cases involving frequent psychiatric or addiction relapses, it may help to teach the family to think differently about progress. For instance, progress can be seen as *longer* periods of *improved* functioning, *fewer* hospitalizations or days in the hospital, and *less severe* substance abuse binges.

Provide a sense of hope. You can do this by discussing the potential benefits of treatment and self-help programs. Reinforce your own willingness to stick with the consumer and her family during rough times.

Help the family prepare for setbacks and relapses. Discuss steps the family can take early in the relapse process before the consumer deteriorates too much. Emphasize that the earlier action is taken, the greater the likelihood that a full-blown relapse can be averted. However, families of people with histories of multiple relapses should prepare how they want to handle serious relapses, including situations in which the consumer refuses all efforts of help. In cases that involve risk of suicide, violence, or severe decompensation, the family needs to know how to initiate an involuntary commitment to a psychiatric hospital so that the consumer gets the help she needs.

CASE ILLUSTRATION 13: WORKING WITH FAMILIES

Joe is thirty-three years old and single. He lives with his mother and father. Joe went to college on an athletic and academic scholarship. During his sophomore year he became very depressed and drifted into alcohol and other drug abuse. He did not return to school for his junior year.

Joe spends most of his time in his room drinking alcohol and listening to music on headphones. Neither his mother nor his father drink alcohol. His mother's religion forbids the use of alcohol. His father's brother and father both died of alcoholism. Joe's father has not had a drink in twenty years. Joe's oldest brother was killed by a drunk driver. His older sister is married to an USAF airman and they live on base in Germany. In the initial family session it was obvious that Joe's father, Hiram, was very angry and frustrated. He had "seen so much destruction from booze" that his son's use of alcohol terrified him. Hiram could not understand why Joe would not "just give it up" like he had.

Joe held tightly to the notion that depression was a disease. He argued that since he had this disease and since antidepressants did not seem to help, he might as well drink. (Joe never took his medications for more than a few days in a row.) Hiram expressed extreme disgust over the notion of depression and alcoholism being called "diseases."

Hiram had led a hard life. Despite all he had been through, he rarely missed a day of work. "Sick is sick," he said. "Lying in bed drunk is not being sick; it's just being lazy. If I laid in bed all day, I'd feel bad about myself too."

Joe's mother, Nancy, tended to play the peacemaker between Joe and Hiram. She spent much of her energy encouraging Joe to do more and trying to convince Hiram that Joe was "sick." Unfortunately, she also spent much of her time enabling. She washed Joe's clothes, made his meals, paid his bills, and occasionally bought him liquor.

The first thing the therapist did was listen. She listened respectfully and asked questions. She gathered information and tried to imagine what it would be like to live in Joe's household.

The therapist then started to teach the family about mental illness, alcohol abuse, and recovery. She quickly discarded the notion that Joe was "hopelessly ill." She agreed that while Joe might have two definite illnesses, both were highly treatable. Joe was not responsible for having them, but he was responsible for doing something about them. It was the family's responsibility to make it tough for Joe to wallow in his illnesses.

The therapist agreed to provide the family with whatever information they needed. They agreed to do the same for the therapist. They agreed to a series of meetings to assess Joe's progress, problem solve, and discuss mental illness, alcohol abuse, medications, self-help groups, and other aspects of treatment.

Initially, Joe continued to drink and refused to take antidepressants. The therapist convinced Hiram and Nancy that while they could not "make" him take the medications, they did have options. After much coaxing, Hiram and the therapist convinced Nancy not to do anything for Joe that a man his age could do for himself. Although neither one of them would agree to attend support groups for families of the mentally ill or alcohol and other drug abusers, they did read many books about addiction and depression. On days when Joe refused to come to the clinic, they came without him. Together they learned not to enable him.

One evening Joe was arrested for being drunk and disorderly. Nancy called the clinician and asked if the clinic could intervene to get Joe out of jail. After much discussion, they agreed that Joe would have to face the consequences of his actions. Joe was released two days later, furious that no one had come to his aid. His mood did not improve when he discovered at his court hearing that his parents refused to pay his fine and, therefore, he would have to perform one hundred hours of community service. The judge also ruled that Joe would have to attend treatment or return to jail.

Reluctantly, Joe started seeing his clinician again, both with and without his parents. After several months Joe began to reveal his frustration with himself. He could remember nothing but success before he became ill and nothing but failure after. Listening to his father get ready for work each morning, he would think about how disappointed his father must be in him.

Eventually he and his father were able to discuss this. They agreed that while the last several years had been painful, the only thing worse would be Joe not changing his lifestyle. An agreement was hammered out in which all parties agreed to attend self-help meetings and counseling. It was made clear to Joe that he would be responsible for his actions and that all enabling would stop.

The Point Is . . .

1. Even if the consumer resists treatment, it pays to involve the family. Helping them can only benefit the loved one.
2. Families need support to break old habits and make tough choices. Sometimes they will feel as if they are abandoning a sick child. Some consumers will play this role perfectly: "How could you leave me in jail, knowing I have depression? What kind of parent are you?" The professional needs to reassure the families that they are doing "the right thing." The professional needs to point out that enabling only makes the situation worse.
3. At times consumers will need help to tell their families how they feel. Hiram had no idea that Joe understood his frustration. Joe was too overwhelmed with guilt to tell him. It is up to the staff member to try to open the lines of communication.
4. Don't paddle away. Teach the family to row.

Sample family psychoeducational workshop

A family psychoeducational workshop is an excellent mechanism for families to learn about mental illness and substance abuse, learn new coping skills, and share support with other families. A variety of formats (half day, full day, two day) can be used. Such workshops can include professionals from various disciplines (psychiatrists, nurses, social workers, counselors, and so on). It helps to have a psychiatrist present for part of the workshop, as clients and families really like the idea of the "doctor" being present, even if other team members do the majority of the work in setting up, recruiting, and conducting the workshop.

Here is one format for setting up and providing a workshop for families of consumers:

Involve consumers. Ask consumers what they want to cover during the workshop. Let them prepare the meeting room, make coffee, or provide snacks. Encourage them to invite family members or significant others to participate.

Invite families directly. Even if the consumers invite their families, you can also invite them to attend with letters or phone calls. A telephone call offers the additional advantage of answering questions and helping families overcome any reluctance they have about attending a family psychoeducational workshop.

Write a one-page flyer describing the program. Post the flyer throughout your unit or clinic and have copies available for consumers and families. Make sure it is attractive and gives a brief overview of the program, including why it is being held, who will conduct it, and what topics will be covered.

Involve different team members. Other team members can help develop the program, present information, and lead discussions. All team members should help recruit consumers and families for the workshop. If the family psychoeducational workshop is not seen as an important service offered by the unit, program, or clinic, its chances of succeeding are reduced. In short, the attitudes and perceptions of staff members are important to the success of the workshop.

Offer food and beverages. If possible make coffee, tea, soft drinks, and snacks available.

Offer families the chance to return for a follow-up session. Follow-up could include additional workshops or individual family sessions to discuss specific concerns or issues.

Provide written information about substance abuse, mental illness, and self-help programs. Pamphlets and booklets on illness, recovery, and support groups are invaluable. The workshop will whet the appetite of many to learn more about their issues. Suggested readings for families are listed in the recommended reading.

Use a variety of methods in the workshop. These include a combination of brief lectures, discussions, question-and-answer sessions, educational videotapes, and comments from other family members in recovery (e.g., members of family support groups such as the Alliance for the Mentally Ill, Al-Anon, or Naranon).

Cover several topics during the family psychoeducational workshop. The topics you cover depend on whether this is a first session or part of an ongoing family program. In general, if families are new to recovery, the following topics should be covered:

- causes and symptoms of psychiatric illness
- causes and symptoms of addiction
- the relationship between mental illness and addiction
- effects of disorders on the consumer and family
- the role of psychosocial treatments, medications, and self-help programs for consumers in recovery
- how families can help their loved one
- how families can help themselves
- ongoing recovery resources for families (professional and self-help)

If you have time, cover other issues to meet the needs of a given group of families.

CHAPTER 14

SUMMARY:
WHAT TO DO

So what are you supposed to do with the consumer who smokes crack and experiences antisocial personality disorder and bipolar disorder and who cannot understand why the world will not change to accommodate him? Let us summarize.

Listen respectfully and you will do more than most people. Listen with two ears. Use one ear to hear the consumer. Why does he believe he cannot get out of bed? What happened to his job? How does the medication make him feel? What is it like to live his life today?

Listen critically with the other ear. Has he not been taking his medications—is that part of the reason he cannot get out of bed? Was he drinking when he lost his job? What does he want that he cannot have because of his mental illness, substance abuse, or both?

Sell him on the idea that he can have some of the things he wants by abstaining from addictive substances and complying with medications. Present the message over and over again no matter what the response. It is vital not to give up too easily.

Circumstances often provide windows of opportunity when consumers are willing to accept ideas they have rejected time and time again. Half the battle is being there when people are willing to consider alternatives—usually after their lives have taken a turn for the worse.

Document those turns. Keep the timeline up-to-date. Talk about each negative event and how it could be avoided. You may want to write down things you disagree on. Focus on factors at the root of the consumer's problem. You may agree on a solution even if you do not agree on a cause.

Confront any use of alcohol and other drugs. Do it gently and matter-of-factly. When someone is intoxicated, do not argue. State your concerns so that you acknowledge an awareness of the problem. The trick is to address the substance abuse without provoking an argument: "You are unsteady on your feet and slurring your speech. I can smell beer on your breath. I am worried about you. The last time you drank beer, you ended up in the hospital." Always use factual statements that show concern. If at all possible, remove any consumer under the influence from your facility.

At the very first chance you get to confront the person while he is not under the influence, update the timeline. Review what happened, why it happened, and what the consequences are. If you do not confront the consumer, you may lose a window of opportunity.

Help consumers use the Twelve Step programs. That may mean discussing the program, taking them to a meeting, or providing in-house alternatives. Sometimes it requires nothing more than encouraging a consumer to continue working at recovery. Your facility should put up a sign with big bold letters that reads, "IT GETS BETTER." Post a list of the AA and NA promises. Display a short paragraph about a consumer who is successfully dealing with his illnesses.

Plan the day. Help a consumer complete a contingency card. Keep track of what works and what does not. Teach him to have realistic expectations. He may believe eating two meals that someone else prepares is a full day. Or he may want to stuff the rest of his life into the next twenty-four hours.

Celebrate small victories. Too often others will measure the consumer's accomplishments solely on the basis of what was done. Look at the situation on the basis of what it takes to achieve the goals. If a depressed consumer drags himself out of bed and gets dressed in time to go to a support group meeting but does not go, celebrate anyway. Consider the effort he has made and highlight that.

Involve families whenever possible. Hold workshops and meet with families individually. Consider families to be a part of the treatment team.

Teach the slogans. The first time a depressed consumer makes it out of bed and downstairs to the kitchen, talk about how he felt. If he is unhappy that he did not make it to the meeting, you can apply some of the slogans:

- *First things first*—He completed several of the steps necessary to get to a meeting. He got up, got dressed, made it downstairs. He put his recovery ahead of his desire to stay in bed.
- *One day at a time*—How far will he make it tomorrow? Ask him how much effort was involved. Point out that two weeks ago he could not have gotten out of bed without help. He is one day closer to feeling better. How does it feel to accomplish at least part of the task? Help him apply the slogans to his life.

CASE ILLUSTRATION 14: DON'T PADDLE AWAY

Tom is a recent graduate of a local university with a bachelor's degree in sociology. He works as a counselor at a drop-in center for the mentally ill. He has read several therapy books but feels that he knows a lot more about theory than practice. He has attended twenty-five AA and NA meetings in the last three months and has started reading the Basic Text of NA. He has a good relationship with Steve, a frequent visitor to the center.

Steve is a thirty-eight-year-old father of two. Until two years ago he worked as a house painter. He was on a scaffold when he had his first panic attack. He immediately got off the scaffold and went to the emergency room. Steve was prescribed Ativan and told that he was suffering from anxiety. When he returned to work the next day, he felt as if he were on the verge of another panic attack. Steve quickly learned that drinking a few beers with his Ativan enabled him to ignore his fears. Six months later he fell off a scaffold and went on disability. His panic spread to several areas of his life, and he found it difficult to leave the house without swallowing a mixture of muscle relaxants, Ativan, and alcohol. He was hospitalized following an apparent suicide attempt. Upon discharge he was referred to the mental health system.

Steve arrived at the drop-in center complaining of back pain. He said he was depressed, that his children were not going to respect him when they grew up and realized he was a "loser." Tom noticed that Steve's eyes were glassy and his speech was slurred. He confronted Steve about this and asked him if he wanted to go to the emergency room or a detoxification center. Steve refused to do either saying he just wanted to watch TV at the center. Tom informed him that he had the option of going to the emergency room or detoxification center but he did not have the option of staying at the center. Steve left angrily saying he knew a bar where he was always welcome.

The next day Steve arrived at the center at noon. He was somewhat disheveled, but his speech was clear and he was steady on his feet. He came in to complain that Tom was "a two-faced college brat" who didn't know what he was doing. Steve implied that he could have died and that all he had asked for was a place to sit until he felt better. He complained that Tom had no idea what it was like to be in pain and permanently disabled. He predicted that if Tom ever found himself in his shoes, he would be depressed and drunk too.

Tom did not interrupt Steve. Steve was not threatening and there was no reason to believe he had been using chemicals. Tom listened respectfully for some time.

From their conversation Tom learned of three things Steve wants that are incompatible with his continued alcohol and other drug abuse. Steve wants the respect of his children, not to be depressed, and gainful employment.

Tom needs to do several things. He has to let Steve know that he is welcome at the center as long as he is sober. He may want to congratulate Steve for arriving at the center sober. He may need to remind Steve why he was asked to leave in the first place. Steve may try to draw Tom into a lengthy discussion about what really happened. If he is smart, Tom will remind him of the rules and move on to discuss other issues.

Next, Tom will want to spend some time discussing what Steve wants and what stands in his way. The cold, hard fact is that drinking is not going to solve any of Steve's problems. In fact, drinking will only worsen the three problems Tom has targeted.

Tom may want to include yesterday's incident on the timeline. Under "consequences," Tom will want to focus on Steve's three issues. He may want to find out if Steve's children saw him drunk and how he feels about that. Was Steve more depressed when he woke up this morning? Did he do anything detrimental to his finding a new career or training?

Tom should try to nudge Steve into applying the slogans to his situation. Steve is sober today; he should begin his recovery again *One day at a time.* If Steve ignores his addiction he will never solve the other three problems, *First things first.* Steve may be able to identify several other slogans that apply.

If Steve is willing to, he and Tom should plan the rest of the day so that Steve does not pick up the first drink. They may want to complete a contingency card. If at all possible, part of the plan should be for Steve to go to a Twelve Step meeting or an in-house group. Steve should inform his psychiatrist that he has been drinking.

It is Tom's job to confront alcohol and other drug use, instill hope, and provide an alternative. Since Tom understands Twelve Step programs and works closely with the community mental health center, he has all the resources he needs to deal with substance abuse and mental illness.

The Point Is . . .

Don't Paddle Away!

APPENDIX I

SELF-HELP PROGRAMS FOR PERSONS WITH DUAL DISORDERS

Double Trouble Intergroup, P.O. Box 2287, Philadelphia, PA 19103. Some AA chapters have special meetings for recovering individuals who have combined alcohol and mental health problems. These groups have a variety of names, according to the area of the country.

Dual Recovery Anonymous, Central Service Office, P.O. Box 8170, Prairie Village, KS 66208, (913) 676-7226. A self-help organization for those with dual disorders (Twelve Step format).

Emotional Health Anonymous, 2420 Gabriel Boulevard, Rosemead, CA 91880, (818) 240-3215. A Twelve Step program for people with psychiatric problems.

Grow, Inc., 2403 West Springfield, Champaign, IL 61821, (217) 352-6989. A self-help program for people with psychiatric problems.

Mentally Ill Recovering Alcoholics (MIRA), P.O. Box 8335, Rolling Meadows, IL 60008.

STEMSS, (Support together for emotional and mental serenity and sobriety), Michael G. Bricker, MS, NCADC, c/o STEMSS Institute and Bricker Clinic, 140 E. Dekora Street, Saukville, WI 53080, (414) 268-0899.

The Steps and Traditions Of Recovery

The Twelve Steps of Alcoholics Anonymous[*]

1. We admitted we were powerless over alcohol—that our lives had become unmanageable.
2. Came to believe that a Power greater than ourselves could restore us to sanity.
3. Made a decision to turn our will and our lives over to the care of God *as we understood Him.*
4. Made a searching and fearless moral inventory of ourselves.
5. Admitted to God, to ourselves, and to another human being the exact nature of our wrongs.
6. Were entirely ready to have God remove all these defects of character.
7. Humbly asked Him to remove our shortcomings.
8. Made a list of all persons we had harmed, and became willing to make amends to them all.
9. Made direct amends to such people wherever possible, except when to do so would injure them or others.
10. Continued to take personal inventory and when we were wrong promptly admitted it.
11. Sought through prayer and meditation to improve our conscious contact with God *as we understood Him,* praying only for knowledge of His will for us and the power to carry that out.

---

[*]The Twelve Steps of AA are taken from *Alcoholics Anonymous,* 3d ed., published by AA World Services, Inc., New York, N.Y., 59-60. Reprinted with permission of AA World Services, Inc. (See editor's note on copyright page.)

12. Having had a spiritual awakening as the result of these steps, we tried to carry this message to alcoholics, and to practice these principles in all our affairs.

The Twelve Traditions of Alcoholics Anonymous[*]

1. Our common welfare should come first; personal recovery depends upon A.A. unity.
2. For our group purpose there is but one ultimate authority—a loving God as He may express Himself in our group conscience. Our leaders are but trusted servants; they do not govern.
3. The only requirement for A.A. membership is a desire to stop drinking.
4. Each group should be autonomous except in matters affecting other groups or A.A. as a whole.
5. Each group has but one primary purpose—to carry its message to the alcoholic who still suffers.
6. An A.A. group ought never endorse, finance or lend the A.A. name to any related facility or outside enterprise, lest problems of money, property and prestige divert us from our primary purpose.
7. Every A.A. group ought to be fully self-supporting, declining outside contributions.
8. Alcoholics Anonymous should remain forever nonprofessional, but our service centers may employ special workers.
9. A.A., as such, ought never be organized; but we may create service boards or committees directly responsible to those they serve.
10. Alcoholics Anonymous has no opinion on outside issues; hence the A.A. name ought never be drawn into public controversy.
11. Our public relations policy is based on attraction rather than promotion; we need always maintain personal anonymity at the level of press, radio and films.
12. Anonymity is the spiritual foundation of all our Traditions, ever reminding us to place principles before personalities.

---

[*]The Twelve Traditions of AA are taken from *Alcoholics Anonymous,* 3d ed., published by AA World Services, Inc., New York, N.Y., 564. Reprinted with permission of AA World Services, Inc. (See editor's note on copyright page.)

The Twelve Steps of Dual Recovery Anonymous[*]

1. We admitted we were powerless over our dual illness of chemical dependency and emotional or psychiatric illness—that our lives had become unmanageable.

2. Came to believe that a Higher Power of our understanding could restore us to sanity.

3. Made a decision to turn our will and our lives over to the care of our Higher Power, to help us to rebuild our lives in a positive and caring way.

4. Made a searching and fearless personal inventory of ourselves.

5. Admitted to our Higher Power, to ourselves, and to another human being, the exact nature of our liabilities and our assets.

6. Were entirely ready to have our Higher Power remove all our liabilities.

7. Humbly asked our Higher Power to remove these liabilities and to help us to strengthen our assets for recovery.

8. Made a list of all persons we had harmed and became willing to make amends to them all.

9. Made direct amends to such people wherever possible, except when to do so would injure them or others.

10. Continued to take personal inventory and when wrong promptly admitted it, while continuing to recognize our progress in dual recovery.

11. Sought through prayer and meditation to improve our conscious contact with our Higher Power, praying only for knowledge of our Higher Power's will for us and the power to carry that out.

12. Having had a spiritual awakening as a result of these Steps, we tried to carry this message to others who experience dual disorders and to practice these principles in all our affairs.

---

[*]Adapted from the Twelve Steps of Alcoholics Anonymous. The Twelve Steps of Dual Recovery Anonymous are used with the permission of the Dual Recovery Anonymous Central Service Office, P.O. Box 8107, Prairie Village, KS 66208. The Twelve Steps are reprinted and adapted with permission of Alcoholics Anonymous World Services, Inc. Permission to reprint and adapt this material does not mean that AA has reviewed or approved the contents of this publication, nor that AA agrees with the views expressed herein. AA is a program of recovery from alcoholism—use of the Twelve Steps in connection with programs and activities which are patterned after AA, but which address other problems, does not imply otherwise.

STEMSS: Support Together for Emotional and Mental Serenity And Sobriety Self-Help Model*

1. I admit and accept my mental illness is separate from my chemical dependency and that I have a dual illness.
2. As a result of this acceptance I am willing to accept help for my illnesses.
3. As a result of this willingness, I came to believe that with help and understanding, recovery is possible.
4. As a result of this belief, I accept the fact that medical management must play a large part in my recovery program.
5. As part of this recovery program, I accept the fact that I must maintain an alcohol and drug-free** lifestyle.
6. In following these steps throughout my life, I will reach my goals and help others to begin the recovery process.

---

*STEMMS: Support Together for Emotional and Mental Serenity and Sobriety Self-Help Model is used with the permission of the STEMMS Institute and Bricker Clinic, 140 E. Dekora St., Saukville, WI 53080. The institute also gives blanket permission to copy, distribute, and/or use their materials for the purpose of starting a STEMSS Group, as long as proper attribution is given. The STEMMS Steps are reprinted and adapted with permission of Alcoholics Anonymous World Services, Inc. Permission to reprint and adapt this material does not mean that AA has reviewed or approved the contents of this publication, nor that AA agrees with the views expressed herein. AA is a program of recovery from alcoholism—use of the Twelve Steps in connection with programs and activities which are patterned after AA, but which address other problems, does not imply otherwise.

**"Drug" refers to recreational chemicals, not prescribed medications.

Schizophrenics Anonymous Steps for Recovery[*]

1. I SURRENDER . . . I admit I need help. I can't do it alone.
2. I CHOOSE . . . I choose to be well. I take full responsibility for my choices and realize the choices I make directly influence the quality of my days.
3. I BELIEVE . . . I now come to believe that I have been provided with great inner resources and I will try to use these resources to help myself and others.
4. I FORGIVE . . . I forgive myself for all the mistakes I have made. I also forgive and release everyone who has injured or harmed me in any way.
5. I UNDERSTAND . . . I now understand that erroneous, self-defeating thinking contributes to my problems, failures, unhappinesses and fears. I am ready to have my belief system altered so my life can be transformed.
6. I DECIDE . . . I made a decision to turn my life over to the care of GOD, AS I UNDERSTAND HIM, surrendering my will and false beliefs. I ask to be changed in depth.

---

[*]Adapted from the Twelve Steps of Alcoholics Anonymous. The Schizophrenics Anonymous Steps for Recovery are used with permission of the Mental Health Association in Michigan, 319 W. Lenawee, Lansing, MI 48933. The Schizophrenics Anonymous Steps for Recovery are reprinted and adapted with permission of Alcoholics Anonymous World Services, Inc. Permission to reprint and adapt this material does not mean that AA has reviewed or approved the contents of this publication, nor that AA agrees with the views expressed herein. AA is a program of recovery from alcoholism—use of the Twelve Steps in connection with programs and activities which are patterned after AA, but which address other problems, does not imply otherwise.

―――――

EXCERPT FROM
THE A.A. MEMBER—
MEDICATIONS AND OTHER DRUGS*

Give the following excerpt (from *The A.A. Member—Medications and Other Drugs: A Report from a Group of Physicians in A.A.*) to consumers to explain A.A.'s official policy on medications. Consumers can then pass it along to people who tell them to stop taking their prescribed psychotropic medication.

At the same time that we recognize this dangerous tendency to readdiction, we also recognize that alcoholics are *not immune* to other diseases. Some of us have had to cope with depressions that can be suicidal; schizophrenia that sometimes requires hospitalization; manic depression; and other mental and biological illnesses. Also among us are epileptics, members with heart trouble, cancer, allergies, hypertension, and many other serious physical conditions.

Because of the difficulties that many alcoholics have with drugs, some members have taken the position that no one in A.A. should take any medication. While this position has undoubtedly prevented relapses for some, it has meant disaster for others.

A.A. members and many of their physicians have described situations in which depressed patients have been told by A.A.'s to throw away the pills, only to have depression return with all its

―――――

*Taken from *The A.A. Member—Medications and Other Drugs,* published by AA World Services, Inc., New York, N.Y., 9. Reprinted with permission of AA World Services, Inc. (See editor's note on copyright page.)

difficulties, sometimes resulting in suicide. We have heard, too, from schizophrenics, manic depressives, epileptics, and others requiring medication that well-meaning A.A. friends often discourage them from taking prescribed medication. Unfortunately, by following a layman's advice, the sufferers find that their conditions can return with all their previous intensity. On top of that, they feel guilty because they are convinced that "A.A. is against pills."

It becomes clear that just as it is wrong to enable or support any alcoholic to become readdicted to any drug, it's equally wrong to deprive any alcoholic of medication which can alleviate or control other disabling physical and/or emotional problems.

REFERENCES

Addenbrooke, W. M., and N. H. Rathod. 1990. Relationship between waiting time and retention in treatment amongst substance abusers. *Drug and Alcohol Dependence* 26:255–64.

Alcoholics Anonymous World Services. 1976. *Alcoholics Anonymous.* New York: Alcoholics Anonymous World Services.

———. 1984. *The A.A. Member: Medications and Other Drugs.* New York: Alcoholics Anonymous World Services.

Anderson, C. M., D. J. Reiss, and G. E. Hogarty. 1986. *Schizophrenia and the Family: A Practitioner's Guide to Psychoeducation and Management.* New York: Guilford Press.

Bogin, D. L., S. S. Anish, H. A. Taub, et al. 1984. The effects of a referral coordinator on compliance with psychiatric discharge plans. *Hospital and Community Psychiatry* 35:702–6.

Brown, U. B., M. S. Ridgely, B. Pepper, et al. 1989. The dual crisis: Mental illness and substance abuse. *American Psychologist* 44 (3):565–9.

Carey, K. B., and M. P. Carey. 1990. Enhancing the treatment attendance of mentally ill chemical abusers. *J Behav Ther and Exp Psychiat* 21 (3):205–9.

Clarkin, J., G. Haas, and I. Glick. 1988. *Affective Disorders and the Family.* New York: Guilford Press.

Daley, D. C. 1988. *Surviving Addiction.* New York: Gardner Press.

Daley, D. C., K. Bowler, and H. Cahalane. 1992. Approaches to patient and family education in affective illness. *Journal of Patient Education and Counseling* 19:163–74.

Daley, D. C., and J. Miller. 1993. *Taking Control: A Family Guide to Chemical Dependency.* Holmes Beach, Fla.: Learning Publications.

Daley, D. C., H. Moss., and F. Campbell. 1993. *Dual Disorders: Counseling Clients with Chemical Dependency and Mental Illness,* 2d ed. Center City, Minn.: Hazelden.

Daley, D. C., and M. E. Thase. In Press. *Dual Disorders Recovery Counseling: A Biopsychosocial Treatment Model for Addiction and Psychiatric Illness.* Independence, Mo.: Herald House/Independence Press.

Gerstley, L., et al. 1989. Ability to form an alliance with the therapist. *American Journal of Psychiatry* 146 (4):508–12.

Green J. H. 1988. Frequent rehospitalization and noncompliance with treatment. *Hospital and Community Psychiatry* 39:963–6.

Hatfield, A. B. 1990. *Family Education in Mental Illness.* New York: Guilford Press.

Hatfield, A. B., and H. P. Lefley. 1987. *Families of the Mentally Ill: Coping and Adaptation.* New York: Guilford Press.

Hochstadt, N. J., and J. Trybula, Jr. 1980. Reducing missed initial appointments in a community mental health center. *Journal of Community Psychology* 8:261–5.

Kadden, R. M., and I. H. Mauriello. 1991. Enhancing participation in substance abuse treatment using an incentive system. *Journal of Substance Abuse Treatment* 8:123–4.

Kaufman, E. 1989. The psychotherapy of dually diagnosed patients. *Journal of Substance Abuse Treatment* 6:9–18.

Keitner, G. I. 1990. *Depression and Families:.* Washington, D.C.: American Psychiatric Press.

Kruse, W. 1992. Patient compliance with drug treatment—new perspectives on an old problem. *The Clinical Investigator* 70:163–6.

Meyer, R. 1986. *Addictive Disorders in Psychotherapy.* New York: Guilford Press.

Miller, W. R., and S. Rollnick. 1991. *Motivational Interviewing: Preparing People to Change Addictive Behavior.* New York: Guilford Press.

Minkoff, K., and R. E. Drake. 1991. *Dual Diagnosis of Major Mental Illness and Substance Disorder.* San Francisco: Jossey-Bass.

Weiner, H., and M. Wallen. 1988. The dual diagnosed patient in an inpatient chemical dependency treatment program. *Alcoholism Treatment Quarterly* 5(1–2): 197–218.

RECOMMENDED READING

American Psychiatric Press. 1994. *Diagnostic and Statistical Manual of Mental Disorders (DSM-IV)*. 4th ed. Washington, D.C.: American Psychiatric Press.

Beck, A. T., G. Emergy, and R. L. Greenberg. 1985. *Anxiety Disorders and Phobias*. New York: Basic Books.

Beck, A. T., F. D. Wright, C. F. Newman, and B. S. Liese. 1993. *Cognitive Therapy of Substance Abuse*. New York: Guilford Press.

Daley, D. C. 1994. *Dual Diagnosis Workbook: Recovery Strategies for Addiction and Mental Health Problems*. Independence, Mo.: Herald House/Independence Press.

Daley, D. C., and L. Bennet. 1992. *Recovery from Psychiatric Illness: A Guide to Psychiatric Hospitalization*. Holmes Beach, Fla.: Learning Publications.

Daley, D. C., and F. Campbell. 1993. *Coping with Dual Disorders: Chemical Dependency and Mental Illness*. 2d ed. Center City, Minn.: Hazelden.

Daley, D. C., and K. Montrose. 1995. *Understanding Schizophrenia and Addiction*. Center City, Minn.: Hazelden.

Daley, D. C., and M. Raskin, eds. 1991. *Treating the Chemically Dependent and Their Families*. Newbury Park, Calif.: Sage Publications.

Daley, D. C., and L. Roth. 1992. *When Symptoms Return: Relapse and Psychiatric Illness*. Holmes Beach, Fla.: Learning Publications.

Daley, D. C., and J. Sinberg. 1995. *A Family Guide to Coping with Dual Disorders*. Center City, Minn.: Hazelden.

Donovan, D. M., and G. A. Marlatt. 1988. *Assessment of Addictive Behaviors*. New York: Guilford Press.

Frances, R. J., and S. I. Miller, eds. 1991. *Clinical Textbook of Addictive Disorders*. New York: Guilford Press.

Glanz, L. 1991. *Overcoming Anxiety and Worry*. Skokie, Ill.: Gerald T. Rogers Productions.

Goodwin, D. W. 1986. *Anxiety*. New York: Oxford University Press.

Goodwin, F., and K. Jamison. 1990. *Manic Depressive Illness*. New York: Oxford University Press.

Haskett, R., and D. C. Daley. 1994. *Understanding Bipolar Disorder and Addiction Workbook.* Center City, Minn.: Hazelden.

Howland, R. H., and M. E. Thase. 1993. A comprehensive review of cyclothymic disorder. *Journal of Nervous Mental Disorder,* 181:485–93.

Kavanagh, D. J. 1992. Schizophrenia. In *Principles and Practice of Relapse Prevention,* edited by P. H. Wilson. New York: Guilford Press, 157–90.

Kreisman, J., and H. Straus. 1989. *I Hate You—Don't Leave Me: Understanding the Borderline Personality.* New York: Avon Books.

Lewinsohn, P., et al. 1986. *Control Your Depression.* New York: Prentice Hall.

Liberman, J. A., J. M. Kane, S. Sarantakos, et al. 1987. Prediction of relapse in schizophrenia. *Archives of General Psychiatry* 44:597–603.

Linehan, M. M. 1993. *Cognitive-Behavioral Treatment of Borderline Personality Disorder.* New York: Guilford Press.

Markway, B. G., et al. 1992. *Dying of Embarrassment: Help for Social Anxiety and Phobia.* Oakland, Calif.: New Harbinger.

Mondimore, F. M. 1993. *Depression: The Mood Disease.* rev. ed. Baltimore: Johns Hopkins University Press.

Pepper, B., and H. Ryglewicz. 1982. *The Young Adult Chronic Patient.* San Francisco: Jossey-Bass.

Rapoport, J. L. 1989. *The Boy Who Couldn't Stop Washing: The Experience and Treatment of Obsessive-Compulsive Disorder.* New York: New American Library.

Salloum, I., and D. C. Daley. 1994. *Understanding Major Anxiety Disorders and Addiction.* Center City, Minn.: Hazelden.

Thase, M. E. 1993. Maintenance treatments of recurrent affective disorders. In *Current Opinion in Psychiatry* 6:16–21.

Thase, M. E., and D. C. Daley. 1994. *Understanding Depression and Addiction Workbook.* Center City, Minn.: Hazelden.

INDEX

abstinence, 17, 21, 24, 33, 38, 66, 75, 83, 105
addict, 74, 93, 104
agoraphobia, 67
Al-Anon, 144
alcohol, 14, 40, 72, 81
    as a self-prescribed anxiolytic, 72
    not treated as a "drug," 17, 41
Alcoholics Anonymous, 47, 60, 128, 130
amphetamines, 14
analgesics, 14
anonymity, 74
anxiety, 11, 14, 72
assessment, 32–47, 82, 142
    families and, 32, 142
Ativan, 67
attitude, 28–29, 38, 48, 49, 52, 68–69, 73, 105
    "being real," 96
    positive, importance of, 38, 49
    staff, 28–29, 48, 52, 68–69, 105
        importance of consistency, 29, 49, 73

barbiturates, 14
beer, 40–41
    not considered "alcohol," 40
benzodiazapines, 23
bipolar disorder, 11, 12–13
    illustrated, 12–13
burnout, 67

celebrating small victories, 24, 38, 67, 155
"check day" habit, 34
clean time, 16, 24, 35
    See also abstinence
cocaine, 14, 16, 40
coffee, 8–9
community resources, 86
compliance, 66, 83
    negotiated, 66
confidentiality, 74
confronting, 49, 52, 53–56, 101, 155
consumers, 50, 66, 68,
    admiration of, 50, 66, 68
    point of view, 72–73
        paradox of, 66
        illustration of, 69, 76–77
contingency cards, 122–125
crack, 17, 38, 64
cravings, 89
    strategies for dealing with, 89–91

delusions, 10, 39–40, 41, 42
    grandeur, 42
    ideas of reference, 10
    paranoid, 42
    persecutory, 10
denial, 39–40, 41, 111, 120
    by definition, illustrated, 39
    timelines and, 111, 120
depressants, 14
depression, 15, 38, 44, 55, 72, 81

ABOUT THE AUTHORS

Kenneth A. Montrose, M.A., is director of training and publications for Greenbriar Treatment Center in Washington, Pennsylvania. Montrose designed a dual diagnosis program at Western Psychiatric Institute and Clinic (WPIC) for consumers with schizophrenia and addiction, and he provided clinical services. He offers dual disorders training programs for professionals and is the co-author, with Dennis Daley, of *Understanding Schizophrenia and Addiction*.

Dennis C. Daley, Ph.D., is an associate professor of psychiatry and chief of Addiction Medicine Services at Western Psychiatric Institute and Clinic (WPIC) of the University of Pittsburgh Medical Center. He has been involved in the treatment of addiction and dual disorders for more than twenty years. Dr. Daley is involved in several research studies sponsored by the National Institute on Drug Abuse and the National Institute on Alcohol Abuse and Alcoholism related to the treatment of co-occurring disorders. Dr. Daley has more than two hundred publications to his credit. His practical recovery materials are used in many treatment programs in the United States and other countries, and several of his books have been translated into foreign languages.